Adventures for (Big) Girls:
Seven Radio Plays

Other anthologies of radio drama
available from Blizzard Publishing

Airborne: Radio Plays by Women, edited by Ann Jansen
Take Five: The Morningside Dramas, edited by Dave Carley

Adventures for (Big) Girls

Seven Radio Plays

Edited by
Ann Jansen

with plays by
Baņuta Rubess / Mary Vingoe /
Carol Bolt / Peggy Thompson /
Beverley Cooper / Linda Griffiths

Blizzard Publishing • Winnipeg

Adventures for (Big) Girls: Seven Radio Plays
first published 1993 by
Blizzard Publishing Inc.
301–89 Princess St., Winnipeg, Canada R3B 1K6

Cover art: *Acrobats Performing in a Meadow* by Ann Smith
Printed in Canada by Printcor.

Published with the assistance of the Canada Council
and the Manitoba Arts Council.

Canadian Cataloguing in Publication Data

Main entry under title:
Adventures for (big) girls
ISBN 0-921368-32-1
1. Radio plays, Canadian (English) – Women authors.*
2. Women – Drama. I. Jansen, Ann. II. Rubess, Baņuta.
PS8309.R34A38 1993 C812'.022089287 C93-098169-3
PR9196.7.R34A38 1993

For Dani, Sarah, Kathryn, Elisa and Rachel
the next generation of adventurers

// Acknowledgments

My thanks to:

All the playwrights, for contributing so generously to this anthology, and in particular to Baņuta Rubess, the source of the series. To Blizzard Publishing's Anna Synenko and Peter Atwood, for their commitment to radio drama and their enthusiasm for these adventures. To Gene Hayden, for her editorial acumen and support. To Neil Besner for his assistance with the Spanish translations. And to Noel Young, of course.

ANN JANSEN

Contents

FOREWORD
by Baņuta Rubess, page viii

INTRODUCTION
by Ann Jansen, page xi

OBLIVION: A STORY OF ISABELLE EBERHARDT
by Baņuta Rubess, page 1

LIVING CURIOSITIES: A STORY OF ANNA SWAN
by Mary Vingoe, page 25

COMPAÑERAS
by Carol Bolt, page 51

CALAMITY JANE AND THE FAT BUFFALO MOON
by Peggy Thompson, page 77

NELLIE BLY: TEN DAYS IN A MADHOUSE
by Beverley Cooper, page 101

THE DUCHESS: PIECES OF WALLIS SIMPSON
by Linda Griffiths, page 125

NO. HERE COMES ULRIKE MEINHOF
by Baņuta Rubess, page 149

Foreword

Adventure books were one of the passions of my childhood. The Hardy Boys and Nancy Drew were nothing compared to the riches I found when my family moved to Germany. I was perhaps ten years old when I discovered Karl May and his fifty books, all of them bound in the dark, purply-green of malevolent bottle flies, the fake-leather covers dappled with fake gold. I collected almost twenty of them.

Although May never left his tiny village, his nineteenth-century imagination stormed through American canyons and Saharan deserts, ducking the blades of enemy pirates. His stoic and noble Indian, Winnetou, was one of the most popular heroes of German fiction. The mental image of Winnetou and his sidekick—his white comrade, Old Surehand—stays with me most vividly now, although May by no means wrote solely about the Wild West. As a ten-year-old, I'm sure I missed all hyper-Wagnerian overtones, all colonial-minded offences. But even then I noticed one terrible absence: my gender.

Women never appeared in the fifty-some volumes, except on the very rare occasion when they had to be saved, swept off a sinking ship or burning roof-top. As I cuddled under the blankets, reliving scenes from my bedtime reading, I would twist and turn the plot so that I could join May's bronzed heroes. I was determined to mount those galloping horses and swing across those swamps on the flaming ropes. Yet I never felt comfortable recast as a man, even mentally. Instead, I'd become a fantastical, asexual Amazon, who by some ultra-daring feat impressed the rest of the boys enough to be one of them.

Eventually, I lost interest. But my buried sense of deprivation flared up again when writing the comedy *Pope Joan* for Nightwood Theatre in Toronto, in 1984. Disguised as a man, Joan snuck through the ranks, as legend had it, to become Pope in the ninth-century. Most versions of the story dwelt primarily on her ignominious death: supposedly she was stoned to death when she went into labour during a papal procession. This was the part of the story most narrators relished: the bloody death of a woman, betrayed by her body. Yet her travels and travails in becoming Pope, her schemes and deceptions during a thoroughly corrupt period of the Holy See, were the stuff of adventure. I chose to ignore the rumours of her death and concentrate on the journey. Even so, I was shocked by the tremendous effort it required to create a female adventurer. I had to consciously break down the social conditioning of my imagination. In the first drafts, the male roles tended to be a lot more fun, a lot more interesting and a lot more active. Somehow my Joan just kept reacting to events, rather than initiating them. Somewhere my conditioning dictated that if she was a hero, it meant she had to be "good"—and "good" meant, basically, sanitized. In other words, boring.

Then one day a girlfriend slipped me a slim volume of stories by Isabelle Eberhardt. Here was a thoroughly unsanitized woman who tested all preconceptions. At the turn of the century, Isabelle disguised herself as a man to kick up the Saharan desert sand on her white horse. Her roguish lifestyle was filled with sex, mysticism, alcohol and drugs—a certain type of romantic ideal. She was definitely *not* a good girl, not a Madame Curie, not even an Old Surehand, but a true rebel. Why had I never heard of her before? Why wasn't she as familiar to me and others as are those other self-destructive poets—those guys, like Rimbaud and Verlaine, or Jack Kerouac. The image of the melancholic and suicidal Sylvia Plath clings to us all, the model of the maligned female victim, but not Eberhardt, with her passion, her confrontational bi-sexual desire, her narcotic and alcoholic abandon, her actions. Her horses! She did not lock herself away and endure. She asked for "it"—over and over and over again. And with the vision of Isabelle, grinning toothless on her white horse, I began to think of adventure stories for women. Unsanitized, and not always pleasant. But with a thrill at the core of every one of them.

Another aspect of that childhood in Germany was the American Forces Network radio. I could read German well enough to devour Karl May, but basically I was a Toronto kid and I tuned in to this all-English-speaking channel every night. Television did not figure in our household, so I was glued to the loudspeaker instead, and it played every version of radio drama recorded. I listened to comedies, mysteries, Westerns, dramas and science fiction. I still get goose bumps remembering some of the evil shadows of the human heart which came with a wallop across the airwaves. The landscape of radio provides great freedom for the dramatic writer's imagination—the locations can be far-fetched and filled with people. Perhaps this is why Isabelle's story suggested itself as a radio play—although I had never written one at that time. I wrote the first draft for the drama, and the idea for the series, in 1985. I wrote it, and left it languishing in my desk drawer.

A couple of years later I mentioned the idea to Bill Lane, an executive producer at CBC, whose own work specialized in the more fantastical regions of radio drama. He seized upon the idea and made it a reality, inviting me to be guest producer of the series at a time when I had never stepped inside a recording studio. He empowered me, pure and simple, and in the process did the same for a number of female writers. Together with Ann Jansen, our script editor, Bill and I spent hours discussing the nature of adventure, questioning our presuppositions. Is the story of a woman who secretly rehearses Shakespeare's *Twelfth Night* an adventure? That of a political terrorist? That of a woman pulled along, unasked, by explorers? As the resulting series proves, our answer was yes. A woman facing danger, or tempting fate, could be an adventurer. Potentially the story of Coco Chanel or Margaret Thatcher could be an adventure. It was all in the telling of the story. Karl May's swashbuckling was left in the dust.

BAŅUTA RUBESS

Introduction

When the radio plays in this collection were first broadcast, they were introduced by a woman's voice announcing "Adventure Stories for Big Girls." But those words on this page don't do justice to the excitement of the beginnings of these adventures. Michelle George *performed* the title; her voice was recorded, electronically treated and repeated. On air, the first few words were straightforward, but the word "big" took on a life of its own. It boomed out, the bass stressed, the word a few sizes larger than average. Then a tiny repetition, this time "big" not as declaration but much more tentative, almost squeaked and tilted into a question. Right after the final "girls," which was stated with a no-nonsense directness, came a voice collage, a kind of scat or sounding, picking up on the words in the title. The voice took off, accompanied by the beat of the series theme music composed by Beverley Johnston. In rapid succession, George lassoed a bunch of unladylike "la la la la la's," tossed in a vamped version of the Tarzan yell and wound up in a crescendo that sounded as if she was headed straight for the stratosphere.

All that from a few simple words.

The irreverence and sense of play let loose in that introduction were wonderfully suited to the series and its take-off title. Both were the creation of Baņuta Rubess, who came to CBC Radio with her idea for a series of biographies of unconventional women. She wrote two of the dramas, commissioned six others, and directed and produced the series. Seven of the plays, which were presented in two seasons on Studio '92 and Studio '93, are printed here (Monique Mojica's *Birdwoman and the Suffragettes: A Story of Sacajawea* is published separately). These plays are adventure stories for grown-ups, big girls and guys. They're about women who stepped out of line and made things happen, women who were out of the ordinary. In fact, one is about a woman who was literally larger than (most) life: Anna Swan was 7'10" tall. As script editor on the series, I was surprised and delighted when the title was so adventurously interpreted, in keeping with the varied styles, humour and sheer zest of the plays.

The adventure stories for girls I read in my youth were much tamer than these dramas. They were about jolly girls in tight corners, Nancy Drews rather than Mata Haris. I enjoyed the derring-do of those girls, the insistence that they could do anything boys could. Of course, the message was typically earnest, and the usual finale was the reward of wife-and-motherhood. At least along the way, the girls got to tame cheetahs or knock out dangerous burglars. The pictures were my favourite part. Here's one story through its captions: "Of all the queer finds"; "My girls on a mountain top"; "Don leaves a letter"; " 'Just lie still and rest,' said Rachel"; "A Wagon Coming up the Trail"; " 'You were only just in time,' she gasped"; and "The rescue."

In these radio adventures, there's no one to come up the trail to make the final rescue, just in time, as girls gasp. The women are moving along the trail themselves, heading for their own adventures. The term adventure is freely defined here. It even encompasses the story of Wallis Simpson, a woman for whom the word "adventuress" evokes its older connotations of a woman who always gets her man—or men—by dubious means. At one point in Linda Griffiths's play *The Duchess: Pieces of Wallis Simpson,* a disapproving crowd member calls the commoner who dared catch a King "a slut, an adventuress." Of course, "adventurer" has been traditionally reserved for men. But in these plays, women make the word their own.

The series includes many women on the move, searching out excitement and fresh experiences, living by their wits. The great, unconventional women in these plays come from different continents and centuries. But they didn't tend to stay put where they were placed. Writer, rebel and Arabist, Isabelle Eberhardt was born in Geneva and died in North Africa. As she said of her chosen climate: "I hate cultivated fields. All that greenery and corn. Melons. Dead landscapes and salty sands, that's more like it." Fenced-in gardens hold no appeal for these women; they are lured by danger and distance. Nova Scotian giantess Anna Swan became an exhibit in P.T. Barnum's New York museum before she took off to see the world. Sharpshooter Calamity Jane was always getting on her horse and riding off to destinations unknown. Karen Ridd left Winnipeg in 1989 to join a peace mission to El Salvador. German terrorist Ulrike Meinhof turned her politics to other ends: she trained as a guerrilla in Jordan and spent the last years of her life underground. Turn-of-the-century New York journalist Nellie Bly once went around the world in less than eighty days, and American divorcee Wallis Simpson ended up far from home after marrying her British prince.

These dramas aren't about every journey these women undertook, every adventure they experienced. The playwrights chose a moment or event in their subjects' lives, rather than striving for the complete story or the last word of a conventional biography. In *Nellie Bly: Ten Days in a Madhouse,* of all Nellie Bly's hair-raising assignments Beverley Cooper focusses on her investigation of Blackwell's Island Insane Asylum. With Anna Swan, playwright Mary Vingoe thought that people put on display might want to seize control, choose their roles and improve upon their audiences. Hence the imagined staging of *Twelfth Night* in Barnum's museum, with Anna cast as director. The subtitles of the plays, "A Story of Isabelle Eberhardt" or "Pieces of Wallis Simpson," for example, clearly indicate the lack of closure in these explorations.

Whether fact or fiction, the chosen event is open to interpretation by virtue of the dramatic form. The plays convey no sense of "the truth"; instead they probe lies, fantasies, mysteries and myths. The playwrights don't promise the whole truth and nothing but … a truth may be all for now. This approach is in keeping with the ways these women interpreted their own lives and became creations of their own making. Some made up the past as well as the future: "I Jane Hickock Burke better known as Calamity Jane of my own free will and being of sound mind do this day June 3, 1903 make this confession. I have lied about my past life … People got snoopy so I told them lies to hear their tongues wag. The women are all snakes and none of them I can call friends." Or Wallis Simpson: "I don't remember any love affairs. One must keep love affairs quiet."

As the Duchess of Windsor, Simpson became a spectacle for society high and low. She and the other adventurers lived very public lives, open to interpretation by all and sundry. Accounts of their doings analyse and explain, but the conclusions are often pat or sensational. Baņuta Rubess's *No. Here Comes Ulrike Meinhof* is a direct challenge to the conventional interpretations of this infamous woman's life. Since her death, Meinhof has been turned into a sideshow; a spate of movies and books have capitalized on her deeds. Rubess brings Meinhof back to life in her play, while parodying these media excesses. The energy, passion—and confusions—of Meinhof's message enter the present tense, and the play bids us think about the costs of consuming lives such as Meinhof's.

According to the hyped docudrama that forms part of *No.*, the German terrorist is virtually unrecognizable after her death. Finally, proof positive comes not from the surface body, the Caesarean scarring common to many women; rather, X-rays are supposed to reveal a wire from a brain tumour operation. It's a wonderful image for the difficulty we have in understanding a woman like Meinhof. The playwrights in this series try to identify what marks their characters, though much less brutally than the Inspector with Meinhof's body. They work from the inside out.

Along the way, the writers have to deal with the adventurers' many guises. These women created a gallery of characters in their own lives, sometimes acting under chosen or assumed names. Eberhardt's passport to another world was her Arabic name, Si Mahmoud. Calamity Jane was a chosen moniker. Nellie Bly, born Elizabeth Cochrane, chose her pen name from a Stephen Foster song when she took her first newspaper job at age eighteen. Only the Duchess changed her family name through the more usual, legal channel: marriage.

If the adventure-story anthologies of my youth held that girls can do anything boys can, sometimes these (big) girls had to dress up as men to get their way. In Peggy Thompson's play *Calamity Jane and the Fat Buffalo Moon,* Calamity Jane is briefly disguised as Wild Bill Hickock in order to fool a Russian duke who wants to hunt with the famous male gunslinger. When the mask slips, Duke Alexis discovers that not only can Calamity shoot as straight as a man (although he himself is a terrible shot), she is "all woman" when they get back to his tent and get into the champagne. The most famous and consistent cross-dresser in this gathering is Isabelle Eberhardt. In *Oblivion,* Rubess explores the story of this white woman who presented herself both as a man and as an Arab. As Eberhardt wrote, "In the staid costume of a European girl I would never have seen anything. The world would have been closed to me, for … external life seems to have been made for man, not for woman."

The plays in this collection explore disguise, the need to mask the selves beneath the public persona. Nellie Bly acts like a madwoman to get the inside story in the insane asylum, only to find herself caught up in her own masquerade. In *Compañeras,* Carol Bolt dramatizes not only Karen Ridd the hero, but also her alter ego, Robo the frightened clown. As well as role-playing as the Duke's nanny in those difficult sexual moments, the Duchess of Windsor acts the part of a queen in exile. In keeping with the way the famous couple was constantly on view, Griffiths has her characters host a long and stylish dinner party. The duo performs a happy-husband-and-wife routine in front of playwright Noel Coward and other guests, but when the door closes behind the curiosity-seekers, their voices are sudddenly devoid of life. In the CBC production,

Griffiths performed the lead role; her characterization included a hyena laugh that constantly interrupted the brittle polish of Simpson's public persona.

Where does the façade end and the person begin? In these plays, only Anna Swan remains determinedly herself, her body precluding any deception. The title of Vingoe's play, *Living Curiosities: A Story of Anna Swan,* highlights the ways women of all sizes have been viewed as "freaks," as "other" than the norm (read "male"). All Anna wants is to be ordinary. She would love to return to Nova Scotia to work as a schoolteacher; for her, the everyday would be an adventure. But she cannot so easily escape being an exhibit in Barnum's grotesque human and animal zoo. Given those circumstances, Anna turns into a director, and the play she chooses is one full of masquerade and gender bending.

Anna has a wonderful group of performers to call on. Sisters Lucia and Alphonsia are cast as the cross-dressed Viola and Sebastian, and the Bearded Lady, Clofullia, takes on the role of Count Orsino. When Clofullia protests that she wants to be seen as a woman, that she has always been mistaken for a man, Anna reassures her: "No, no, no. Don't you see, Madame Clofullia? You are showing them your true spirit. You are in control now. It doesn't matter that you are a man or a woman, but that you are a breathing, loving, passionate person. What they saw as a deformity is transformed into beauty and they will listen to you as they never have before."

These radio plays ask us to listen to these women's lives as we never have before. Radio is known for its ease in rewriting the bodies behind the words. The actor's appearance doesn't matter in the least. On radio, we know Anna only through her voice, and she comes across as a charming, educated and personable woman. Size is irrelevant except as it relates to the drama of her life. On air no one is a "freak." We can *hear through* to the person; we remain responsible for choosing the characters' disguises and placing their masks.

Radio drama is also in the forefront of colour-blind casting. For *Compañeras,* Alison Sealy-Smith, a black actor perhaps best known for her role on the television series *Street Legal,* was cast both as Karen Ridd, who is referred to in the script as a tall blonde gringa, and as Robo, her male clown. The script steers us to picturing Karen's height and blondness, but with Robo we're on our own. In the same play, Daysi, a Salvadoran character, was played by a white actor named Alisa Palmer, whose "Spanish" speeches were all in fluent English. When she was supposed to be truly speaking English to an uncomprehending Karen, her speeches were delivered with a Spanish accent.

One of the economies of the medium is to have actors perform more than one role, and in that case the voices must be distinct for each character. Often cross-casting and role playing is "behind the scenes," inaudible to the listener. But in these plays, individual characters are sometimes intentionally masked. When a character assumes a disguise on radio, the audience has to be let in on the trick. So when Calamity Jane impersonates Wild Bill Hickock, the audience is made aware of the joke—only the Duke is being duped. Radio drama is the perfect place for shape-shifting of all kinds. In taking full advantage of that freedom, the playwrights challenge our conceptions of the roles women play, on air and off.

Radio drama is all about transformation. The translation of the words of the series title into its layered musical and vocal presentation is just one example of the shift that happens when interpreters get together to translate a script into sound. Not every change between page and air is that dramatic, but the words do call out for interpretation. The script acts as a blueprint for the final layering of voices, sounds and music, translated from the page by the producer, performers, sound effects technician and composer. Radio drama is technological storytelling, and almost every sound, including actors' voices, is electronically manipulated and treated, whether during recording or in post-production. Nonetheless, for all that sound is the medium, radio drama is an oddly visual art form.

Words and sounds must be translated by the audience into mental images for both characters and circumstances. Carefully designed performance and technical choices along the way certainly shape the final imaginings. However, all the pictures of people and places are ultimately left up to us, the listeners. We decide just how tall Karen Ridd or Anna Swan is; we set the scene for the shootouts and the seductions. The Nefta and Batna that Isabelle Eberhardt yearns for are real places; they are also open to our imaginative claim because their essences are communicated through music and sound. In our culture of relentless visuals, radio drama returns us to the story and lets us form our own images. Like both the listener and the producer (radio's term for the director), in this anthology you, the reader, are invited to imagine the ways sound effects and music combine to create a space for the story.

Turning these scripts into radio for the CBC productions usually involved only a week in studio. In some cases, a rehearsal was held, particularly when there were specific acting challenges, such as the clowning in *Compañeras* or the society chorus in *The Duchess*. Then the soundtracks were laid down one by one. A day was spent on cast recording, scene by scene, another on sound effects, and a third on music, with the last two days spent mixing all the recordings.

Original music, created for the dramas by different composers, sets a stamp on each play. The musical choices for the series were as varied as the adventurers, ranging from Lesley Barber's calliope theme for *Living Curiosities* to the haunting wind instruments of Eberhardt's desert theme, composed by Nic Gotham. In some cases, the music themes incorporate other sounds, such as the electronic static that fades in and out through *The Duchess.* Picked up from the bad telephone connections early in the play, the buzz and crackle continue to underscore the difficulty of communication throughout the relationship. And the play's music is another way of telling the story: New Orleans jazz jousts with a Victorian theme, "Yankee Doodle" versus "There'll Always Be an England." Similarly, in *Nellie Bly: Ten Days in a Madhouse,* an optimistic big city jazz gives way to gothic, eerie tones as the intrepid (big) girl reporter goes from the newsroom to the asylum.

Of all the sounds in a play, characters are the easiest to track, both on the page, because their dialogue is laid out, and over the air, because characters are identified primarily through voice, whether inner or outward. Some also have sound tics or are signalled by musical themes during intense moments. Robo's signature theme was composed of words, music and sounds. The clown's sirens, bells and whistles worked with a made-up language to form an ongoing private drama that turns public. Although the dialogue for Robo's clown language and suggested sound effects were written by the playwright, the final mixture of voice and noisemaking were improvised by the performer, Robo's emotional jangle a tailored counterpoint to Ridd's surface calm.

For more realistic elements of the dramas, the recording is designed to situate characters physically for the listener. Although the actors are gathered around the microphone, their characters are heard sitting, walking, running and struggling. The fishbone scene in *The Duchess* and the slapstick struggles between Aziz and Abou in *Oblivion* are examples of complex, choreographed sound, in which the characters are clearly in motion. Yet through all the activity, the actors work in relation to a still centre, the microphone.

Characters who remain silent for too long disappear on radio and so they are often identified through sounds other than words. Even when characters aren't identified as speaking on the page, they may be making appreciative or disbelieving noises, sucking on a cigar or causing a chair to creak. Although some of these sounds are designed after the fact by the sound effects technician, others are created by the performers. The clinking glasses of the ousted royal couple's dinner party were affected by the actors, whereas Anna Swan's creaking chair came later.

Most of the scenarios are built up after the fact of the voices, layers of sounds added to create the overall effect, as well as specific signifiers for individual characters. Sound effects for characters and scenes tend to be of two sorts; they either form part of an ongoing ambience or act as specific phrases in the drama. While sound effects signalling particular moments and events are indicated in the script, they may not occur in the recorded drama exactly as marked. When a scene opening indicates the use of coyotes, crickets or camp-fires to establish a night setting, some of the sounds will probably be constant, while others will punctuate the dialogue. A distinct coyote howl isn't just thrown in, it's carefully chosen to fit a charged moment. In Rubess's production of *Compañeras,* the second time an interrogating official abruptly kills a buzzing, irritating fly is a shocking moment, carefully timed and executed. And during Ridd's interrogation, the clock ticks more loudly during her internal monologues, underlining the subjective nature of time during her prison ordeal.

In addition to "real" spaces, a train moving across buffalo-crowded Western plains or a dank and horrible washroom in an insane asylum, radio provides other, imaginary places from which characters can speak. Special treatments are designed in studio to make voices differ for narrations or internal monologues, referred to as "Internal" in the script. These conventions give us first-hand access to the viewpoints or musings of a character. One of the great pleasures of radio drama is its intimacy, the way the voices in the play speak just for us, whether seductively whispering in our ears or insisting we sit up and pay attention. Radio is the perfect medium for eavesdropping, either listening "in" on a crowd or entering a single character's dreams or waking thoughts.

The lines between all these perspectives are easily blurred. Robo the clown is a fiction, playing inside Ridd's head, but his responses to El Salvador become more and more perceptive. At one surreal point in *Compañeras,* Robo merges with another character, a grief-crazed woman prisoner, and the convenient line between self and other is shaken. *Oblivion* also weaves together realistic and imagined voices. As with *Compañeras,* the main character has two internal voices, and they also enter into a dialogue. But in Rubess's play, no clear character line is drawn between these two voices, although they are identifiable both by sound and spoken intentions. The resulting duel between aspects of Eberhardt's inner life is fascinating. As well, the child Isabelle appears twice as if in a vision to speak with the elder Isabelle. Narrative choices in the play include Eberhardt speaking her thoughts aloud and setting the frame for her own fiction. Other characters report on her death by drowning in the desert. When Eberhardt is asleep or unconscious, we hear as she hears, as if through a bell jar or underwater. And the drug-inspired reveries, as well as a dream frame, add to the sense of the permeable line between real and conjured.

These plays are not only adventure stories, they're also *about* the process of making up adventures as you go, and telling the stories later. In addition to her many labels (vagabond and voluptuary, "La Belle Nomade" and "The Amazon of the Sands"), Eberhardt was indubitably a writer. Rubess dramatizes a fragment of one of Eberhardt's works of fiction, a fantasy of domination that depicts a woman named Rakhil overpowered by a man. Unlike Rakhil, Eberhardt constantly makes her own choices, designing her own life, although within some difficult parameters. Nellie Bly actually writes a script for her life, though her style is less literary, more yellow journalism. She constantly files news reports in her head, accompanied by grandiose headlines to match her daring exposés-to-come. But her self-aggrandizing certainty and journalistic fervour desert her when she is trapped in a world where she has no control. The line between third-person reports and first-person fear is crossed in the insane asylum. Her words fail her.

Even though the record may not always match the reality, the characters seem compelled to keep notes on their lives. The plays are replete with letters from mothers and return post from daughters. In dramas where the words aren't written down, the process of interpretation is still clear. In *Compañeras,* Ridd's descriptions of events are counterpointed by Robo's very different running commentary, which exposes the undercurrents beneath the surface. *The Duchess* is another play where appearance and reality are out of joint. Unlike the other adventurers, Simpson doesn't communicate outside the action of the play. Instead, playwright Griffiths created a "society chorus" to spill the gossip about this woman who was very much in the public eye. Only at the end of the play does the title character speak directly for once, an attempt to answer the question that haunts the entire drama: did she love her prince?

The final play in this anthology comments very specifically on the process of making things up, biography as well as radio drama. In *No. Here Comes Ulrike Meinhof,* a conventional, melodramatic radio docudrama on Meinhof's life is interrupted when the activist materializes in Studio G, the Toronto radio studio where these plays were recorded. The line between real and imagined is given an additional twist in this play. During her visit, Meinhof confronts another "real" woman, this time still living. That character is a CBC Production Engineer named Joanne. Playwright Rubess actually based the character on a woman named Joanne Anka, who is a CBC Recording Engineer. Then, as producer, Rubess cast Anka for the role. Anka's name is frequently heard on the credits of CBC's radio dramas, but this was the first time she was listed as a performer. In *No.*, Meinhof's theories blind her to the realities of the woman in front of her—she can't see past her obsessions, her own mythology.

Meinhof insists that Joanne halt the overdone broadcast about her life. When she shouts that the drama is a crime, Joanne attempts to appease her by saying, "I guess the writer got the facts wrong." The exchange continues:

ULRIKE: Facts are irrelevant. The people need the truth.
JOANNE: I work on so many of these dramas I don't even listen anymore. It's up to the producers to check the facts.
ULRIKE: Not the facts, the truth.
JOANNE: But the facts are the truth.
ULRIKE: *This* is the truth ...

Of course, Ulrike's interpretation of reality is up for questioning in this drama, as are the truths and imaginings of the other adventurers.

Part of the truth is that the adventures of these and other women still need to be told. We need to listen to women having their own adventures. In her recent book *Arguments with the World,* Bronwen Wallace refers to a report on government-approved reading materials in Ontario schools. In the textbooks studied, women performed 15 tasks, in comparison with men, who took on 45 different activities. The report noted that "Women's tasks included being a loyal friend, eyeing a letter suspiciously, bossing neighbours, and being sick with a headache. Men's tasks included investigating a kidnapping, acting in silent films, operating a restaurant chain." The conclusion: "... most female adventures involved watching others have adventures, being captured and not surviving." These findings were based on textbooks being read *now,* by girls and boys in grades four, five and six.

This anthology is a way of keeping these adventures alive in a world where most stories feature women still reading those letters left by Don, waiting for someone to come galloping up for the rescue. In these stories, (big) girls are writing the letters, the newspaper reports, the fiction, the plays, the lives. And the adventure doesn't end with the plays' broadcast or publication. As each drama concluded on air, Michelle George returned to announce the following week's adventure. At the end of the series, her last words were: "Next week's adventure will be your own."

ANN JANSEN

Oblivion

A Story of Isabelle Eberhardt

by

Baņuta Rubess

Oblivion: A Story of Isabelle Eberhardt was commissioned by the Canadian Broadcasting Corporation for Studio '92, and first broadcast on the CBC Stereo network on January 17, 1992, with the following cast:

Brenda Robbins (Isabelle)
George Seremba (Bartender / Old Man)
Oliver Dennis (Messenger / Aziz / Lyautey)
Lisa Yamanaka (Little Girl)
Gina Wilkinson (Rakhil / Natalie)
Marlow Vella (Boy)
Guillermo Verdecchia (Slimène / Si Abdesselem / Doctor)
Hrant Alianak (Ahmed / Tidjani)
Damon D'Oliveira (Abou / Officer)
Alison Sealy-Smith (Mother / Servant)

Directed in Toronto by Baņuta Rubess. Produced by Studio '92 Executive Producer Bill Lane. Original music by Nic Gotham. Casting Consultant: Linda Grearson. Recording Engineer: Joanne Anka. Sound effects by Bill Robinson. Production Assistant: Kate Nickerson. Script Editor: Ann Jansen.

Introduction

Isabelle Eberhardt (1877–1904) was one of the last nineteenth-century wanderers and romantics. She was born in Geneva. Her mother was a Russian aristocrat who had run off with her children's tutor, a bearded nihilist. In 1887 Isabelle and her mother embraced Islam and moved to North Africa. After her mother's death, Isabelle spent the rest of her short life travelling the Sahara on horseback dressed as a man. Known as Si Mahmoud, she spoke six languages, including several North African dialects, and was initiated into the Qadrya, a Sufi brotherhood. Her life was a series of exotic adventures and misadventures. Through Islam, she searched for oblivion, expressed as the union with the Absolute; through drugs, drink and men, she searched for oblivion through the flesh. She was respected for her piety and knowledge by the native North Africans, and was derided by most of the French colonials. Colonel Lyautey valued her as a correspondent and a go-between among various tribes. She worked as a journalist and a writer of short stories, some of which have been translated by Paul Bowles.

As is logical in a life rife with contradictions, she married a man with half her zest for the unconventional, Slimène. At twenty-seven, already sick, she joined him in the village of Aïn Sefra. When a freak flood rushed through the town, she drowned in the desert. The French Legionnaires picked her scattered writings out of the mud and sent them to Paris, where they were at first published under a male pseudonym.

As I mentioned in the foreword, the story of Isabelle Eberhardt kicked off the idea for the entire series. She is by no means a positive role model—thank God. Instead she satisfies the realm of the forbidden imagination. Her love affair with hallucinations dictated the fantastical narrative of the adventure I wrote.

BAŅUTA RUBESS

Characters

ISABELLE: Isabelle Eberhardt
BARTENDER
MESSENGER
RAKHIL: A beautiful Jewish girl
SI ABDESSELEM: A great Moroccan magician
AHMED: A desert Sufi
AZIZ and ABOU: Ahmed's nephews
LITTLE GIRL
SLIMÈNE: Isabelle's husband
BOY
OLD MAN
MOTHER
TIDJANI: An assassin
SERVANT
DOCTOR
NATALIE: Isabelle's half-sister
LYAUTEY: A colonel in the French Legionnaires
OFFICER

Oblivion

A Story of Isabelle Eberhardt

Scene One: Café

(MUSIC: "Isabelle" theme, North African instruments, underneath.)

(SOUND: Dogs barking, El Oued marketplace in the distance, underneath. ISABELLE snores.)

(MUSIC: Out.)

BARTENDER: Wake up, Si Mahmoud.

(SOUND: Slaps.)

Wake up.

(SOUND: ISABELLE groans.)

MESSENGER: *(Slightly off.)* Sheikh Sidi Lachmi is waiting.

BARTENDER: Sheikh Sidi Lachmi is waiting for you. Pull up your red boots and greet the sun.

(SOUND: ISABELLE mumbles.)

(To MESSENGER, politely.) I have been trying to rouse him all morning, sir.

MESSENGER: Sheikh Sidi Lachmi leaves for Nefta within the hour. The camels, the guides, the guns, they have all been assembled.

BARTENDER: Sometimes it helps if you put a cushion over their face, want me to do that? They can't breathe and they wake up very quickly. Or not at all.

MESSENGER: Sidi Lachmi sings his praises. But here he lies, under the table!

BARTENDER: Oh, but this is no common wretch, sir. Si Mahmoud is a writer!

MESSENGER: A scribbler—

BARTENDER: A patriot of North Africa! All France reads his reports from the Sahara!

MESSENGER: French swine!—

BARTENDER: He is a student of Islam, of classical calligraphy.

(SOUND: MESSENGER grunts grudging approval, continuing underneath.)

He speaks French, German, Arabic, Greek, Latin—*and* every desert dialect! They say he cured the children in Amiche of the red pustules.

MESSENGER: Yes, yes, quite admirable. But the pilgrimage must leave *now.*

(SOUND: ISABELLE groans and coughs disgustingly.)

BARTENDER: I could sit on his chest, want me to do that? Then they think the house has collapsed and they confess all their sins.

MESSENGER: Just shake him a bit, can't you.

BARTENDER: I'm afraid he'll be in no shape for riding. He's had a pail of absinthe and a pouch of strong kif *[cannabis].*

(MUSIC: "Kif" theme begins underneath.)

(SOUND: ISABELLE groans.)

ISABELLE: *(Internal and over.)* Kif, sweet kif ... yellow smoke ... narcotic smoke ... the magic horizon ...

(SOUND: Slaps.)

BARTENDER: Wake up, wake up.

ISABELLE: *(Internal.)* Oh, Slimène, darling, you're such a brute.

BARTENDER: Opp! There goes his turban!

MESSENGER: Now you've done it!

BARTENDER: A thousand pardons, Si Mahmoud.

(SOUND: ISABELLE sighs.)

(MUSIC: "Kif" theme out.)

MESSENGER: Wait a minute ... it can't be ... goodness, man, that's a woman.

(SOUND: ISABELLE murmurs and laughs.)

BARTENDER: We don't like to think of it that way.

MESSENGER: But it is in fact a woman! Dressed as a man—dressed as an Arab—

BARTENDER: It would be rude to draw attention to a circumstance which Si Mahmoud has chosen to disregard.

MESSENGER: But—I—

BARTENDER: Very rude.

MESSENGER: The caravan will stop for twenty-four hours in Behima. Perhaps "he" can meet us there. Allah ma'at. *["Allah be with you."]*

(SOUND: Awkward steps.)

(Moving off.) Never in a thousand lives would I have thought ...

(SOUND: MESSENGER stumbling over a dog, the dog barking, MESSENGER cursing.)

Scene Two: Café

(MUSIC: Music which feels like a hangover.)

ISABELLE: *(Internal.)* The floor is so cool against my cheek as the carpet revolves like Galileo's universe. So cool. My cheek. Against his copper ass. Slimène, your ass, it's like the floor of a squalid café. Cool. Hard. That time in Paris, too, Abdulaziz, his thighs like stones, roof beams crashing in on me as he pressed me on my back. Paris ... I still had my teeth then ... Isabelle, "la belle nomade," the latest toy for the jaded salons, ohlala, and she dresses like a man you know ... *(She groans; internal continues.)* My breath ... it stinks ... there is a dagger in my head.

(MUSIC: Hangover out.)

(SOUND: A splash of water, then busier market sounds, continuing underneath. BARTENDER laughs.)

(Spluttering.) Chto! *["What!"]* Quoil! *["What!"]* Khalifa! Couldn't you just shake me like a regular shit! I could have drowned!

(SOUND: The scrape of a chair.)

Where is everybody? What time is it? Did Slimène go home without me?

BARTENDER: It is the afternoon and Sergeant Slimène has left for Batna.

ISABELLE: Batna! That stinking vomitory! But why? He didn't tell me he was planning to—Batna! The garrison town! The worst! When is he coming back?

BARTENDER: Never. The French military authorities have transferred Sergeant Slimène to Batna. For good. They left at the crack of dawn. And Sheikh Sidi Lachmi left on the pilgrimage to Nefta. He sent a messenger, but you would not awake. You have been sleeping all day long.

ISABELLE: Sheikh Sidi Lachmi! The holy man! I am a fool, such a fool. I'm leaving for Nefta at once.

BARTENDER: It is good you don't go to Batna.

ISABELLE: I *must* go to Batna at once! Slimène! In Batna!

BARTENDER: Si Mahmoud. It is not good for Slimène, this liaison. You are a foreigner … and you are … different … You know the authorities have objected to this … friendship.

ISABELLE: The pigs, they won't get rid of me so easily. I'm going to Batna at once.

BARTENDER: But Sheikh Sidi Lachmi expects you in Nefta.

ISABELLE: Batna, Nefta …! Let me enter the Sahara and the answer will be clear.

(SOUND: Door opens. The market louder.)

(MUSIC: The blinding sun.)

My head, there is a dagger in my head.

(MUSIC: Up and then down underneath.)

Scene Three: On the Dunes

(SOUND: A galloping horse.)

ISABELLE: *(Internal.)* Nefta … Batna … Batna … Nefta … the spirit or the flesh … How dare the authorities interfere, we're not living in the 1800s any more … this isn't some town in Brittany, this is Africa! When, oh when, will my fellow beings stop persecuting me? I dress as a man, so I can mount my horse Souf with ease. As an Arab, because I belong to Islam. To smoke kif and spit blood with the nomads and the Legionnaires. But those imbecilic, neurotic Europeans, they don't understand. "How stupid and blind men are, slaves of people and things." Alone, I am free … free to—

(SOUND: Horse stops.)

(Internal.) What's that? Something on the distant horizon … across the stones … Innahā mashī'at‿u‿llāh. *["Allah has decided."]* *(Aloud.)*

Souf! We've caught up to the Sheikh. Nefta. I'm going to Nefta. Nefta. The world of the spirit. Allez, allez, allez!

(SOUND: Horse whinnies. Galloping up a hill, stopping.)

Whoa!

(SOUND: The wind, for a moment.)

(Internal.) Nothing. No one. An illusion.

(MUSIC: Piercing tones, like the burning sun.)

(SOUND: Crunching sand, the horse walking slowly, ISABELLE limping and breathing heavily, all underneath.)

(Internal.) The sun smites you like a sword. Then the pain falls away for a moment, like a black web across the eye, false shadow, just to store up your strength for new suffering. Like the struggles to the surface of a drowning man.

(MUSIC: More piercing tones.)

(SOUND: ISABELLE vomits. The wind rises, a whinny. A sandstorm grows, underneath.)

Souf, my ivory darling, don't be afraid. Poor beastie, the blood keeps coming from your parched nostrils. Souf, you must learn to enjoy it. Like me. When I suffer, I begin to live.

(MUSIC: Tones.)

(SOUND: The sandstorm increases underneath.)

(Internal.) A wall of sand … a wall of sand … fills your mouth and eyes like shame.

(MUSIC: A final piercing note.)

(Internal.) This is the end … Isabelle-Wilhelmina Marie Eberhardt, born 1877 of Russian anarchists in Geneva, a journalist, a hedonist, a diplomat, died in 1901 a free spirit wandering the Great Land of Thirst … Mektoub! Kamā yashā'u llāh. *["As Allah desires."]*

(SOUND: The sandstorm blows over her.)

Scene Four: A Dream

(MUSIC: Unearthly, introducing a fantasy, continues underneath.)

ISABELLE: *(Narrating.)* Once in these parts there lived a beautiful Jewish girl, Rakhil, who came to the great magician Si Abdesselem the Moroccan for help.

(SOUND: Wash of the sea, continuing underneath.)

RAKHIL: *(Sobbing.)* I'm in love with a man who is cruel. He's left me. Tell me if he's coming back.

ISABELLE: *(Narrating.)* For a long time Si Abdesselem made figures and letters on a wooden writing board.

(SOUND: Scratching on a board.)

SI ABDESSELEM: You'll pass an hour of delight and high hopes with him. Then you will die in your own blood.

ISABELLE: *(Narrating.)* The girl rolled on the rug, sobbing.

RAKHIL: Why should I die? I'm young. I want to live.

ISABELLE: *(Narrating.)* Si Abdesselem felt no pity. Was not everything that was to befall her already written, and thus inescapable? And was it not a sign of her ignorance that she would lament the fact that her life was to be out of the ordinary? After all, she would know more intensity and passion than most mortals, and she would be spared boredom and disgust.

SI ABDESSELEM: You'll pay me what I ask?

RAKHIL: Yes, if it's not too much.

SI ABDESSELEM: Then I'll take what I want.

(SOUND: Struggle.)

RAKHIL: Let me go! I'm not for you. Let go of me. Take your hands off my breasts.

(SOUND: Clothes ripping.)

SI ABDESSELEM: A ripe pomegranate on the ground. Whoever picks you up can have you. What a man finds is a gift from Allah.

RAKHIL: No! No!

(SOUND: Cries of gulls and the sea, growing underneath.)

ISABELLE: Yes! Yes! Pin me to the ground. Bitter and brutal. I like it that way. I'll pin you to the ground. To roll in the black mud of the gutter.

(MUSIC: Out abruptly.)

Scene Five: Near the Well

(SOUND: Night in the desert, wind, a trace of crickets, underneath.)

ISABELLE: *(Waking up with a start.)* Hello? Where is everybody? What time is it? *(Spitting and spluttering.)* What? I'm in my grave. Up to my neck in sand. Drowning in desert.

(SOUND: Scrabbling out of deep sand. ISABELLE grunts, then a snort of laughter, then disgusting coughing that stops abruptly.)

Oh no. Souf! Souf! He's gone.

(SOUND: Jackals at a distance.)

Alone. Without a horse. I'm carrion.

(SOUND: A distant whinny.)

Souf, you wizard! You found some bushes!

(SOUND: Running, stumbling steps, crickets getting louder.)

(Panting.) What is your bloody nose into? Water! Water.

(SOUND: She falls on her knees and starts to drink.)

(MUSIC: A surge of teasing, tickling wind instruments.)

AHMED: *(Close.)* Stop! Whaddya think you're doing?

AZIZ and ABOU: Yeah, whaddya think you're doing?

ISABELLE: I … I was drinking. *(Internal.)* The black turbans!

AHMED: Did you have our permission?

(SOUND: Jangle of daggers.)

ISABELLE: Brother, I nearly died just now. *(Internal.)* Marquis de Morès was murdered here.

AHMED: Who're you calling brother?

AZIZ and ABOU: Yeah, who?

ISABELLE: Perhaps, perhaps I spoke too soon. *(Internal.)* They never found his assassins.

AHMED: You speak our language, but your face is pale. Are you a Moslem?

AZIZ: He's a thief.

ABOU: He's a spy.

AZIZ and ABOU: He's looking for someone.

(SOUND: Scuffle.)

AHMED: *(Choking ISABELLE.)* Have you come with the French to conquer us?!

ISABELLE: *(Coughing.)* I have powerful friends.

AZIZ: Who is going to find you?

ABOU: A black vulture from hell. *(Nasty laughter.)*

AHMED: What's this? A necklace?

(MUSIC: Far-off sacred air.)

(SOUND: Beads clicking. ISABELLE, released, taking deep breaths.)

(Over.) The black prayer beads of the Rose of Baghdad. He belongs to the Qadrya. A Sufi. A brother. Poor devil. Have a drink, friend. Call me Ahmed, and these two scoundrels are my nephews, Aziz and Abou Naddara.

(SOUND: ISABELLE collapses and drinks noisily.)

(MUSIC: Rises, a bridge to next scene.)

Scene Six: By the Fire

(SOUND: Faint night creatures. A fire crackles nearby, underneath a general grunting and smacking of lips.)

ISABELLE: When I first saw you … those black turbans … I thought you were Touaregs … or even Tidjanis …

AHMED: No, we're not Tidjanis. They'd have killed you on the spot. They hate the Qadrya.

ISABELLE: I know. They say the Tidjanis killed Antoine de Vallombrosa, the Marquis de Morès.

ABOU: Hacked him into bits.

AZIZ: The Tidjanis stop at nothing.

ISABELLE: But they never found the assassins. There's a big reward for their capture.

AHMED: God has already punished them, brother. He has taken their wives and driven them into the wilderness.

ISABELLE: The reward is thousands of francs.

(SOUND: Sucking fingers, underneath.)

AHMED: Life is a sad burden and we must make the best of our destinies. You are safe with us, brother, sleep here by the fire. Aziz will stand guard.

(SOUND: A gunshot. A whinny.)

AZIZ: Shit! I did it yesterday.

ABOU: No, you didn't.

(SOUND: Another gunshot. Another whinny.)

You try this every night. It's a waste of bullets.

AZIZ: My finger slipped.

ISABELLE: Where's the target?

AZIZ: Right here. I'm lighting my cigarette.

ISABELLE: With a pistol shot? *(Beat.)* I see, with a pistol shot.

(SOUND: Another gunshot. A more frenzied whinny. Sounds of appreciation.)

AZIZ: Almost.

ISABELLE: Very close.

AZIZ: Now you try, brother. Take my pistol.

ISABELLE: All right.

AZIZ: Put the cigarette in your mouth.

ABOU: Blow off your nose!

(SOUND: Pistol hammer clicks back.)

ISABELLE: Like this?

AZIZ: Take good aim.

ABOU: Put a big hole in your face.

ISABELLE: A valuable gun. With your initials inscribed.

AZIZ: Just light the cigarette.

(MUSIC: Slides underneath.)

ISABELLE: "A." "V." Aziz Vee—

ABOU: Just light the cigarette!

ISABELLE: Ahmed Vee—

AZIZ: Shoot!

ISABELLE: *(Internal.)* Antoine de Vallombrosa! The Marquis de Morès! They did him in! My brothers—assassins!

(MUSIC: Peaks and out.)

(SOUND: A gunshot. The most frenzied whinny. Sand scattering. Shouts of triumph.)

AZIZ: See! It worked! And it makes for an excellent smoke!

ISABELLE: Yes, brother. Thanks. I was lucky, al-Ḥamdu lillāh. *[“Thanks to Allah.”]*

ABOU: He's a better shot than you.

AZIZ: No he isn't. Shut up.

(SOUND: ABOU and AZIZ have a fist-fight, rolling off into the desert.)

(MUSIC: Tickling wind instruments, underneath.)

ISABELLE: *(Internal.)* The reward would feed me for a year. But there's three against one. But I'm a better shot. But they're your brothers in the Qadrya. Better to sleep. Sleep? With these three? Better to ride away in the night! *(Whispers.)* Souf. Souf!

(SOUND: The horse clip-clopping slowly. AHMED snoring, moving off.)

ABOU: *(Moving off.)* Where did he go?

AZIZ: *(Moving off.)* I don't know. You insulted him!

ABOU: *(Moving farther off.)* No I didn't.

AZIZ: *(Moving farther off.)* Yes you did!

(SOUND: Fist-fight continues, moving farther and farther off, then fades underneath.)

(MUSIC: "Isabelle" theme, a bridge to next scene.)

Scene Seven: Salt Flats

(SOUND: Horse stops. Wind and the cry of a jackal in the distance and underneath.)

ISABELLE: The salt flats. A horizon-less, milky sea, studded with small white islands. This way to Batna. That way to Nefta. It is not for me to decide. Alhimnī yā Allāh. *["Allah, send me a sign."]*

(MUSIC: An apparition, underneath.)

LITTLE GIRL: Who are you?

ISABELLE: Who are you? *(Silence.)* Don't be shy, little girl. What pretty tattoos you have on your forehead. Where did you come from? *(Silence.)* When I was your age, they didn't let me past the gate. Who lets you wander in the desert?

LITTLE GIRL: You do.

ISABELLE: I had nothing to do with it.

LITTLE GIRL: What are *you* doing here?

ISABELLE: I'm a vagabond. The vagabond owns the earth. If you can be free of all things and all people, you are the richest man in the world.

LITTLE GIRL: I'm not a man.

ISABELLE: Tell you a secret. Neither am I.

LITTLE GIRL: No. You are Isabelle Eberhardt.

ISABELLE: How did you know?

(MUSIC: The apparition out.)

Where did you go?

LITTLE GIRL: *(Very close.)* Isabelle!

ISABELLE: A vision. Qāla‿llāh. *["Allah has spoken."]* I am Isabelle, the woman, Isabelle … This means the flesh, this means Batna. Batna, Batna!

(MUSIC: "Isabelle" theme, rises, swells, then out.)

Scene Eight: Corridor and Apartment

(SOUND: Running up the stairs, insistent knocking. SLIMÈNE's racking cough, off and muffled. The door creaks open.)

ISABELLE: Slimène! Surprise! I'm here!

SLIMÈNE: Si Mahmoud! I thought I'd never see you again.

ISABELLE: Ba'atha liya‿llāh. *["Allah sent me."]* I have saddle sores for you.

(SOUND: The door closes. Rustle of an embrace, moving to mattress.)

SLIMÈNE: You stink of sweat! Mmmmm, you stink. I've missed you so much. *(Kisses her repeatedly.)* We will make love like sad devils and then you must go, my flower, my falcon, my fox.

ISABELLE: What?!

SLIMÈNE: I can't let you stay here, Mahmoud. I am trying to get somewhere in this world. Look at me! Born an Arab, but now I wear a French uniform.

ISABELLE: Don't be ridiculous!

SLIMÈNE: Be reasonable, my sweet. Or I'll throw you against the wall.

ISABELLE: You'll be sorry if you do.

SLIMÈNE: I've been sick! We didn't get to know each other in good times.

ISABELLE: Slimène! Pull yourself together.

SLIMÈNE: Don't scold me. You're my wife.

ISABELLE: Yes, certainly, I am your wife. But I am not just a vulgar Fatma. I am also your brother Mahmoud. Can't we make love? I'm aching for you.

SLIMÈNE: Yes, beloved. Come here.

(SOUND: Unbuckling of belt, rustle of clothing and creaking of mattress.)

ISABELLE: *(Nuzzling up to him.)* Treat me like a man … a woman … whatever you prefer …

SLIMÈNE: *(As he buries his face in her neck.)* And afterwards, farewell.

ISABELLE: No! *(Her protest is muffled by a kiss.)*

(SOUND: Kissing, panting and lovemaking mingling.)

(MUSIC: A "Love Rut" theme rising to a crescendo and then petering out.)

Scene Nine: At the Table

(SOUND: A bottle is uncorked, absinthe is poured into glasses, clinks. Drinking with contented sighs.)

SLIMÈNE: They'll never give you permission to stay in Batna. They think you're a British spy. They don't like you. They don't like you at all. They're probably arranging your expulsion from Algiers this very minute.

ISABELLE: Then there's only one solution. We must kill our ourselves tonight.

SLIMÈNE: I'm not ready for that.

(SOUND: A match is struck.)

ISABELLE: *(Toking.)* No? Two dead lovers lying in the moonlight, belly to belly, while a soft warm wind blows in their hair. With no earthly cares and vanities to trouble them—?

SLIMÈNE: *(Toking.)* Your eyes are shining most unnaturally.

ISABELLE: And if I did it alone—could you continue without me? In Batna? Without me? Without me forever?

(SOUND: Another match struck.)

SLIMÈNE: All right. Tonight. In the palm grove.

ISABELLE: Yes?

SLIMÈNE: Yes.

ISABELLE: Then hurry. Wax your moustache, I'll grab the absinthe.

SLIMÈNE: You bring your gun and I'll bring mine.

(MUSIC: A solo instrument, sly and insinuating, a bridge to next scene.)

Scene Ten: Palm Grove

(SOUND: Night creatures, underneath. ISABELLE hums tunelessly.)

SLIMÈNE: *(Reciting from the Koran.)* "In the Gardens of Delight, therein they shall recline upon couches, there will wait upon them youths who will not age—"

(SOUND: A match is struck.)

ISABELLE: *(Toking.)* Never!

SLIMÈNE: "They carry goblets filled with ever-flowing wine, no headache will they get therefrom—"

ISABELLE: *(Exhaling.)* None!

SLIMÈNE: "… nor will they be intoxicated—"

ISABELLE: Paradise!

(SOUND: Clink of a bottle.)

Empty. No more absinthe.

SLIMÈNE: But there is plenty of kif left.

ISABELLE: I met a little girl … Slimène! My life has been essentially sad. Since the beginning. And forever.

SLIMÈNE: After tonight, you will never be sad again, my love.

ISABELLE: We will die like men. I will shoot you through the heart. Then put the gun in my mouth.

SLIMÈNE: *I* will shoot you first. Then I'll shoot myself.

ISABELLE: We will shoot together. Like brothers. Like Russians.

SLIMÈNE: Ouch, my ribs, you're poking too hard.

ISABELLE: Kiss me.

(SOUND: They tumble on the ground. A gun goes off. Screams, silence. A dog barking.)

(Laughing.) I thought *I* was dead.

SLIMÈNE: Uh oh.

ISABELLE: Slimène. You can't pass into the Beyond in that condition.

SLIMÈNE: Look who's talking.

ISABELLE: Your pants are wet.

SLIMÈNE: Just let me lie here for a minute. *(Starts to snore.)*

ISABELLE: Slimène. Slimène, don't fall asleep on me. *(Sighs.)* I'm such a squalid creature. A wretched dog. I don't deserve to die. Astaghfiru‿llāh. *["Allah forgive me."]* I've smoked too much kif today. This countryside stinks. I hate cultivated fields. All that greenery and corn. Melons. Dead landscapes and salty sand, that's more like it. *(Sudden sobs.)* When, when will I find that far off Thebes, where I shall escape at last from the idiocy of my fellow creatures? Where my senses will at last cease to trouble me? Where I will be one with the Absolute? This is all I ever wanted.

(SOUND: Enormous rushing of water, a bridge to next scene.)

Scene Eleven: Desert

(MUSIC: "Isabelle" theme, fading.)

(SOUND: Horse coming to a stop. Wind, the cry of a jackal in the distance, underneath.)

ISABELLE: The salt flats. A horizon-less milky sea, studded with small white islands. This way to Batna. That way to Nefta. It is not for me to decide. Alhimnī yā Allāh. *["Allah, send me a sign."]*

(MUSIC: An apparition, underneath.)

LITTLE GIRL: Who are you?

ISABELLE: Who are *you? (Silence.)* What are you doing here?

LITTLE GIRL: Searching.

ISABELLE: For what?

LITTLE GIRL: Nothing.

ISABELLE: Is that what you want?

LITTLE GIRL: Nothing.

ISABELLE: What's to become of you?

LITTLE GIRL: Nothing.

ISABELLE: What's your name?

LITTLE GIRL: Si Mahmoud.

ISABELLE: But that's impossible.

(MUSIC: The apparition out.)

Hey, where did you—?

LITTLE GIRL: *(Very close.)* Si Mahmoud!

ISABELLE: Nothing. Nothing. Si Mahmoud. Qāla͜llāh. *["Allah has spoken."]* A mystery pointing to the Absolute. The pilgrimage. To Sheikh Sidi Lachmi. To Nefta.

(SOUND: Galloping.)

(MUSIC: "Isabelle" theme.)

Scene Twelve: In Town

(SOUND: An agitated crowd of people in the distance. Closer, whinnies and dismounting.)

ISABELLE: Boy—hey—where can I find Sheikh Sidi Lachmi?

BOY: The pilgrimage? In the house over there by the square.

ISABELLE: Where the people have gathered around the well? Why are all those people—

(SOUND: A group of clamouring boys rushes by.)

BOY: *(Moving off.)* Wait for me!

ISABELLE: … all those people looking down the well?

(SOUND: Steps towards crowd.)

Hey! What tragedy is here? Did she lose her necklace in the well?

OLD MAN: Ai, she is crazy, she has lost her head. She thinks she'll find her daughter down there.

MOTHER: Taalith jumped in the well, I know she jumped in the well.

OLD MAN: How would you like that for a mother-in-law. Taalith was to marry me three days ago and then she disappeared.

MOTHER: In the well!

OLD MAN: Eh, she ran away with the servant boy.

(SOUND: Groans of people pulling up a heavy bucket.)

ISABELLE: There's something down there all right.

(SOUND: Groans of disgust at the sight of a drowned corpse being pulled from the well.)

MOTHER: Taalith, my darling! Taalith!

ISABELLE: *(Internal, over.)* Your heavy wedding jewels! Your coral bridal crown! Your silver girdle!

(SOUND: Crowd takes sides; MOTHER striking OLD MAN.)

MOTHER: *(Weeping.)* She's dead, she's dead, you ugly, old goat of a bridegroom! Taalith, Taalith!

MESSENGER: *(Close.)* You must be Si Mahmoud.

ISABELLE: How did you know?

MESSENGER: I saw you before, in El Oued. I am a servant of Sidi Lachmi.

(SOUND: Crowd gets louder then fades.)

Scene Thirteen: Quiet House

(SOUND: Fountain, birds, steps on marble.)

MESSENGER: We feared the Tidjanis had ambushed you.

ISABELLE: *(Weak.)* I am so happy to be here.

MESSENGER: The trip was too hard—

ISABELLE: No, no, it was that corpse. Is there any death worse than drowning?

MESSENGER: Yes, such a sight is hard on a woman.

ISABELLE: Excusez-moi?

MESSENGER: Ah … young woman wedded by force to an old man, jumps in the well, nothing unusual, I'm afraid. Lillāhi fī khalgihi shu'ūn. *["Allah's ways are mysterious."] (Moving off, calling.)* Seddik! Some tea for our guest. You will feel better soon.

ISABELLE: May I see Sheikh Sidi Lachmi?

MESSENGER: Ah, so unfortunate, he has retired for the night. We continue to Nefta at dawn. You should bed down as well, Si Mahmoud. *(Moving on.)* But there is one thing …

ISABELLE: What is it?

MESSENGER: There are some telegrams, some commercial concerns, a pettiness … but there is no one to translate and by tomorrow we must reply … I understand you speak French?

ISABELLE: But of course.

MESSENGER: *(Calling.)* Seddik! Pen and paper for our guest. *(To ISABELLE.)* A thousand thanks, Si Mahmoud.

(SOUND: Shuffle of papers.)

When you are finished, I will show you your quarters. Excuse me. *(Muttering under his breath, moving off.)* He is not a woman and I must stop thinking about it!

(SOUND: Door closes, off. Rustle of papers.)

(MUSIC: Creeps underneath.)

ISABELLE: "The price quoted here is …" *(Internal.)* Did I ride for two days through a sandstorm for this? A telegram from some fat businessman in Marseille, some shitting ass of a spotted dog? *(Aloud.)* Why did I have to arrive just then … *(Narrating.)* Taalith … Now she knows the ineffable joy of death … *(Internal.)* But to drown … *(Narrating.)* Allah alone knows what is hidden in the sky and the earth! *(Internal.)* These telegrams are idiotic. *(Aloud.)* "The hundredweight of wheat bundles finds with forty-percent of …" *(Internal.)* Gobbledygook!

(MUSIC: Tightens underneath.)

TIDJANI: *(Panting.)* I don't know you, I bear no grudge against you, but I have come to kill you.

ISABELLE: "Forty-percent of all bundles of wheat will be deposited in the harbour of—" *(Internal.)* The grammar is excruciating—

(MUSIC: A sudden, very high note.)

(SOUND: Calls of "Watch out!" "Guards!" "Si Mahmoud!" etc. ISABELLE is hit by a sabre from above. Groans, screams and shouts.)

What? *(Internal.)* It's an earthquake. *(Aloud.)* Stop! *(Internal.)* He's trying to cut my head off!

TIDJANI: What does it take to kill you, you devil. Get me a gun!

(SOUND: Scuffle.)

SERVANT: I've got you now, you scoundrel!

(SOUND: TIDJANI screams; TIDJANI struggling. Running steps, moving on.)

MESSENGER: *(Moving on.)* Si Mahmoud, are you all right?

ISABELLE: Am I dead?

SERVANT: The sabre was deflected in the last minute by that laundry line.

ISABELLE: Almost dead?

MESSENGER: Tidjani scum.

DOCTOR: We'll be able to save your arm, I think …

BOY: He crept up behind him. A Tidjani. But a pink cloud descended upon Si Mahmoud and hid him from the assassin and the blow missed its mark.

DOCTOR: Undo the robes.

(MUSIC: Shock.)

SERVANT: Look! Allah has turned him into a woman.

(SOUND: Crowd gasps in wonder.)

TIDJANI: Allah told me to kill you.

ISABELLE: This is a sign. A sign of my destiny. I am to be holy.

TIDJANI: You're an offence to Islam. I had to kill you. Allah told me.

MESSENGER: More likely, there is some other conspiracy behind this.

ISABELLE: I forgive you, Tidjani. Nothing happens by chance in this world, Lillāhi‿l-ḥamd. *["Thanks be to Allah."]* "My life is a dream." *(Sighs.)*

(SOUND: A thud, a gasp from the crowd. Slapping.)

MESSENGER: Si Mahmoud. Wake up, Si Mahmoud. Wake up.

Scene Fourteen: Dream

(SOUND: Sinking, tinkling noises pulling ISABELLE into a vortex of memory and premonition.)

LITTLE GIRL: *(Far off.)* Wake up Si Mahmoud!

ISABELLE: Oblivion … oblivion … the mysterious blue wall … past the gate … Who wants to stay in the tangled garden?

(SOUND: Carriage on cobblestones, bell tinkling, then out.)

NATALIE: *(From a distance.)* Sick of it, sick of it, sick of it …

ISABELLE: *(Over.)* Geneva … empty dark house … sister run away …

(SOUND: Isabelle's mother weeping.)

(Over.) Brother Nicholas gone to Russia … don't cry, mother.

NATALIE: *(Close.) Your* father, not mine.

ISABELLE: Vladimir killed himself why—

NATALIE: *(Fading up.)* … crazy house and all the crazy people in it—

ISABELLE: Don't die mother, don't don't die, I can't—

(SOUND: The crowd in Nefta, with slaps.)

MESSENGER: Wake up, Si Mahmoud!

(SOUND: Crashing water.)

(MUSIC: "Isabelle" theme, getting stronger, underneath.)

ISABELLE: *(Narrating.)* Oblivion. Worship the hallucinating smoke. Dream-palaces … dream-voices … dream-thoughts …

SLIMÈNE: *(Rapturously.)* "Toi, toi, O! avec toi, toujours—toujours avec toi, de près ou de loin, toujours."

ISABELLE: Slimène—Slimène, hold me! Slimène, my husband …

(MUSIC: "Isabelle" theme out.)

SLIMÈNE: *(Flatly.)* They are sending me to Aïn Sefra.

(SOUND: Crashing water.)

Scene Fifteen: Montage

(SOUND: Typewriter.)

OFFICER: October 21, 1904. Aïn Sefra. Closing the file on Isabelle Eberhardt.

LITTLE GIRL: Wake up, Si Mahmoud!

LYAUTEY: You can imagine how saddened I am by the loss of our poor Isabelle Eberhardt. I have sent my Legionnaires to rake through the mud for scraps of paper with her handwriting. We will send what we find to the publisher in Paris.

ISABELLE: *(Narrating.)* Batna. Nefta. Aïn Sefra.

(MUSIC: The blinding sun, underneath.)

SLIMÈNE: The weather was clear and there was neither rain or storm. We heard a rumbling sound. The mass of water arrived in the bed of the ravine in an instant; it rose up like a yellow wall; it ran like a galloping horse; it was carrying trees and furniture, bodies of animals and men.

(SOUND: People running by, exclaiming with fear, horses galloping, water rumbling.)

(MUSIC: "Isabelle" theme, riding over the water.)

ISABELLE: *(Narrating.)* Nefta or Batna. Flesh seeking flesh. Spirit seeking spirit. The search for oblivion.

(SOUND: LITTLE GIRL laughs.)

(SOUND: Typewriter.)

OFFICER: She was twenty-seven.

(SOUND: Water, building underneath.)

ISABELLE: Is there any death worse than—

(SOUND: Sudden silence.)

SLIMÈNE: She drowned in the desert. There is no other God but God and Mohammed is his Prophet.

(MUSIC: "Isabelle" theme, calm and beautiful, underneath.)

ISABELLE: *(Narrating.)* "In the morning the west wind arrived suddenly. You could see it coming, raising high spirals of dust, black as smoke. As it moved towards us through the calm air, it made great sighing sounds. And then it was howling like a living thing. I had a fantasy of being lifted up and carried off in the enormous embrace of a winged monster, come to destroy us all. And the sand showered onto the terraces with the steady, small sound of rain."

(SOUND: Soft waves crashing, continuing.)

(MUSIC: "Isabelle" theme, underneath.)

(SOUND: Slaps.)

BARTENDER: Wake up, Si Mahmoud. Wake up.

LITTLE GIRL: *(Distant.)* Wake up, Isabelle. Wake up.

ISABELLE: There is no other God and Mohammed is his Prophet. Mektoub! It is written.

(MUSIC: Rises. The end.)

Living Curiosities

A Story of Anna Swan

by

Mary Vingoe

Living Curiosities: A Story of Anna Swan was commissioned by the Canadian Broadcasting Corporation for Studio '92, and first broadcast on the CBC Stereo network on January 31, 1992, with the following cast:

Anne-Marie MacDonald (Anna)
Peter Blais (Barnum)
Ted Dykstra (Zip / Eng / Guard / Gent)
Kevin Frank (Harris / Chang / Edwards)
Guillermo Verdecchia (Man / Jones)
Alison Sealy-Smith (Lucia / Lady Two)
Jenny Dean (Clofullia / Nurse)
Gina Wilkinson (Alphonsia / Mother / Lady One)

Produced and directed in Toronto by Baņuta Rubess. Original music by Lesley Barber. Casting Consultant: Linda Grearson. Recording Engineer: Glen McLaughlin. Sound effects by Jean Sarrazin. Production Assistant: Kate Nickerson. Script Editor: Ann Jansen. Executive Producer of Studio '92: Bill Lane.

Introduction

I was about ten when I first became aware of Anna Swan. I remember being taken to the Halifax Citadel for a school outing. There she was, along with Giant McAskill, two huge wooden statues with hands outstretched to greet us at the entrance of the tiny museum inside the barracks. These life-size carvings were a tribute to Nova Scotia's nineteenth-century fame as a land of giants. There were rumours that Angus McAskill and Anna Swan had been romantically linked but it had not gone well and she had ended up marrying a giant from Kentucky. McAskill had died tragically at home in Cape Breton. To my ten-year-old mind this was exotic stuff. A few years later the statues disappeared.

Some twenty years later while working at the Ship's Company in Parrsboro, I passed through Tatamagouche on a postering drive. What better place for a poster than the local museum. I walked in expecting to stay only a moment and there she was, or at least her dresses, her shoes, her hats, gloves, jewellery and a substantial photographic display from her days of glory at Barnum's New York Museum and from her later tour to meet the crowned heads of Europe. Anna Swan had not been entirely forgotten by her native province. Here in this small town not far from her birthplace of New Annan, she was still remembered.

Anna Swan was born in 1846, the third of twelve children, to a poor family in Colchester County. By the time she was four she had reached the height of 4'6", by the time she was seven she was taller than both her parents. By virtue of her height she was to have an extraordinary life. She was to be famous, wealthy and a traveller, things completely impossible to a girl of her background had she been of normal height. And yet the price she paid for this was to agree to being an exhibit, an attraction to divert the general populace from its own woes. How did this intelligent young woman cope with this?

Research led me into the world of Barnum's museum in the 1860s. This was a kind of gallery of natural wonders, freaks and oddities, an early ancestor of today's science centre, zoo and amusement hall combined. Barnum knew that people loved to be duped, amazed and startled. He knew that controversy sold tickets; he was perhaps the greatest publicist of all time. He felt no qualms about exploiting the public's credulity, nor did he waste time on the inner feelings of the "freaks." How did Anna, all of seventeen and fresh from Teacher's College, react when she first went to New York? Did she feel herself to be a freak, did she come to align herself with the other "living curiosities"? We don't really know, we just know that after the fire of 1865 she left Barnum and went on to tour Europe and the United States. This play is fiction, although the characters are not. *Living Curiosities* is the story of Anna Swan as I have imagined her, have been imagining her since I met her at the Halifax Citadel back in grade five.

MARY VINGOE

Characters

ANNA: Anna Swan

NURSE

HARRIS: An associate of P.T. Barnum

LADY ONE, LADY TWO and GENT

BARNUM: P.T. Barnum

ZIP: "The Missing Link"

GUARD

MAN

MOTHER: Anna's mother

LUCIA and ALPHONSIA: "The Albino Twins"

CLOFULLIA: "The Bearded Lady"

ENG and CHANG: "The Siamese Twins"

EDWARDS and JONES: Barnum's men

Living Curiosities

A Story of Anna Swan

Scene One: Hospital Room

(MUSIC: "Intro" up.)

(SOUND: Rustle of skirts, water pouring from a jug into a basin. Hushed whispers around the bedside: "There she is," "She seems to hear us but doesn't respond," "It's like a coma," "We're not sure," etc.)

(MUSIC: "Intro" out.)

NURSE: Miss Swan, Miss Swan. Can you hear me?

ANNA: *(Internal.)* A hospital bed … I'm in a hospital …

NURSE: I'm putting some water here beside you … do you have the strength to drink it?

ANNA: *(Internal.)* Nursing sisters in white, whispering among themselves …

NURSE: We've never seen anything like it … you inhaled a great deal of smoke.

ANNA: *(Internal.)* … washing my forehead … my hands with damp towels.

NURSE: You're lucky to be alive.

(MUSIC: Slides in underneath.)

ANNA: *(Internal.)* I'm lucky … lucky … that's what Harris said to me when he brought me to New York.

(MUSIC: Up for next scene.)

Scene Two: Horse-drawn Carriage

(SOUND: A New York street, 1862: carriages, street vendors, etc.)

HARRIS: You're a very lucky girl, Miss Swan. Mr. Barnum will make you famous.

ANNA: I want to go home.

HARRIS: Now Miss, we've come all this way and Mr. Barnum's paid our fare … your parents would be terribly disappointed if you turned back now. Watch your step. Let's try and get in quickly so we don't attract a crowd of onlookers, quickly now, come on …

(MUSIC: Up and then down underneath.)

Scene Three: Barnum's Gallery

(SOUND: Lions, elephants, etc. A gaggle of "oohs" and "ahhs.")

LADY ONE: *(Forced whisper.)* The giantess! There she is …

GENT: What a size! Imagine taking that one on. *(Laughs.)*

(SOUND: Laughter among the men.)

LADY TWO: Think how much she must spend on a single dress. *(Titters.)*

HARRIS: *(Moving slightly off.)* This way Miss Swan.

(MUSIC: Out.)

Scene Four: Barnum's Office

(SOUND: A door opens, then closes, muffling sounds from the gallery. A swivel chair creaks.)

BARNUM: Well, Harris, you outdid yourself this time! Why madame, bless me if you aren't eight feet tall! Miss Swan, you are worth every dollar I paid to bring you here.

HARRIS: I've got a few more receipts sir, little costs we didn't anticipate.

(SOUND: A match is struck.)

BARNUM: *(Puffing on a cigar.)* You know, Miss Swan, Harris has brought me a few interesting specimens in the past. The Aztec children, the Hungarian minstrels were yours, eh Harris, but now you, a genuine Canadian curiosity! Why madame, forgive me if you do not weigh over four hundred pounds!

ANNA: *(Hesitantly.)* You should know, Mr. Barnum ... that my true height is only seven feet, ten inches—not the eight feet, one inch, that Harris has led you to believe.

BARNUM: Ah, that's nothing of importance.

ANNA: There's something else. I have been attending Teacher's College in Truro and intend to return there as soon as circumstances allow.

BARNUM: Indeed? Excellent! Perhaps you can inject some discipline into our unruly public.

ANNA: My family is in some financial difficulty at the moment that requires me to be here. I'm sure it will be only temporary.

BARNUM: Well, well, I'm sorry to hear that, Miss Swan. But you can think of this as your home for the time being. One thousand dollars a month and your board and lodging. What will they think of that back home in Nova Scotia? More money than they've ever heard of. They'll be happy if their young giantess does a striptease for that, eh? Scots, I suppose, your people? *(Beat.)*

ANNA: From the Hebrides.

(SOUND: A drawer is jiggled open and paper removed.)

BARNUM: I must write away there, see what else they can send me. *(Little laugh.)* Now Anna, if you'd like to sign here, you'll find yourself well provided for.

(SOUND: Paper crackle.)

ANNA: It says here I must pay you one half of all the anticipated gate receipts if I leave before two years is up.

BARNUM: I invest a great deal of money in my properties, Miss Swan.

ANNA: I can't stay that long.

BARNUM: Then you have a choice, Miss Swan. You can turn around now and go back to Canada, or join me on my own terms. *(Pause.)* Harris will show you to your room, should you decide to stay. Up next to the albinos, Harris, and don't forget to show Anna the fire escape. We had quite a little scare the other day ... ahem.

ANNA: Perhaps I'll just sit down for a moment.

BARNUM: Don't sit on any of these chairs! I mean ... they're meant for the public ... *(Little laugh.)* ... not for a girl your size.

ANNA: I'm sorry.

BARNUM: There's a few things you'll have to learn, if you stay with me. Never show yourself outside the museum unless I've agreed to it and never be late to exhibit. Don't say anything controversial to the public, I handle all that, and no alcohol on the premises. This is an upright American establishment. I've never had any trouble with giants in the past, not like the dwarves and midgets, so I won't expect any with you. *(A little chuckle.)*

(MUSIC: A teasing "Living Curiosity" theme slides underneath.)

You are a splendid curiosity, Miss Swan. *(Moving off.)* Yes, I'm sure you'll do fine.

(SOUND: Door opens and closes.)

ANNA: I can't stay here, Harris, not for two years!

HARRIS: Look Anna, you might have a few rough days at first, but once you make a few friends in the museum, you'll find it easy enough.

ANNA: I don't wish to talk to anybody, least of all his other "interesting specimens."

HARRIS: You don't have to say much … come on, sign the contract.

ANNA: I suppose they would not want to see me back home now.

HARRIS: They need the money, Miss Anna.

(SOUND: ANNA signs the contract.)

That's a good girl. Come on now, have a look in the gallery. It's after closing.

(MUSIC: Swells underneath.)

ANNA: *(Internal.)* Two years! How was I ever to last that long?! Surely I could never be at home in P.T. Barnum's gallery of freaks, along with the wild animals, the Feejee Mermaid, the Siamese Twins, the Bearded Lady, the Albino Twins …

(MUSIC: "Living Curiosity" theme out.)

Scene Five: Barnum's Gallery

(SOUND: Caws of exotic birds, monkeys, rustling in cages, elephants.)

ANNA: *(Reading.)* "Lucia and Alphonsia di Lugar, from Madagascar. Negro sisters who through a miracle of nature have been born with ice white skin" … Huh. Doesn't look like anybody's home. *(Pause.)* Oh God, this one's alive! It looks like some sort of baboon, poor wretched thing.

(SOUND: Scrabbling in sawdust, clinking and rattling of metal.)

Come here fella, here you go boy …

ZIP: *(With a raspy twang.)* Miss Swan?

(MUSIC: Sting: a surprise.)

ANNA: Ah, ahaahaaa … what are you?

ZIP: The name's Zip.

ANNA: What?

ZIP: Your ears not working properly? Zip! Z. I. P. Real name's Henry Jackson.

(MUSIC: Underneath.)

ANNA: *(Internal.)* I had never seen a creature so ugly. His head was so small, it looked squashed. And his face so disfigured … I really took him for an animal.

(MUSIC: Out.)

ZIP: Welcome to the American Museum.

ANNA: What are you?

ZIP: *(Moving off.)* The Missing Link.

(SOUND: Clink and clank of brass rings, trapeze swinging, wild cawing of bird.)

ANNA: What?

ZIP: *(Moving in cage.)* That's what I'm billed as, the missing link between man and the apes … a black dwarf with a cone-shaped skull, it was the best name they could find for me. Coined by Sir Charles Dickens himself on his first visit to the museum. Made Mr. Barnum very proud. Ten years and they still haven't found me out. Of course, they will … the day I die, and he turns my body over to science.

ANNA: What!

ZIP: The learned professors will denounce me as a fraud and Barnum will get lots of publicity. He'll charge the public twice as much to tell them how he fooled the scientific community.

ANNA: That's barbaric.

ZIP: That's the way it is.

(SOUND: A horse whinnying.)

ANNA: That horse looks as if someone stuck sheep's wool all over it.

ZIP: They did.

ANNA: Why?

ZIP: Barnum's "Woolly Horse," captured in the rocky mountains.

(SOUND: More whinnying and shuffling of hooves.)

ANNA: I don't believe that for a minute. Look at the poor creature. He won't live long like that.

ZIP: I'll take him down to the stables in a minute. All the animals are kept in the basement at night.

ANNA: I think it's criminal to dupe the public. There are enough oddities in the world, I'm sure, without having to invent them.

ZIP: What are you doing here?

ANNA: What do you mean?

ZIP: You can't stay here and not dupe the public. You're a freak. You have to stand there and pretend you like being stared at. You don't kick them in the teeth—which is probably what you will want to do.

ANNA: I am not a freak!

ZIP: Excuse me, madame.

ANNA: I'm sorry … I just wasn't expecting … do you just stand there in that case, and let people stare at you?

ZIP: Do I have a choice? Do you?

(MUSIC: Swells, a bridge to next scene.)

Scene Six: Full Gallery

(SOUND: Shuffle of feet, sounds of menagerie. Excited whispers of crowd as they file in to see ANNA. Remarks like "extraordinary" and "astounding" are interspersed with cruder comments such as "Wouldn't she be a handful now?" and "Take a look at those dugs.")

GUARD: *(Over crowd.)* Move along, please. This way, madame.

MAN: What are you wearing under that skirt?

ANNA: *(Internal.)* Please, please, make him go away.

GUARD: Move along now.

MAN: What's under the skirt, big lady?

ANNA: *(Internal.)* Stay calm. Just don't say anything.

GUARD: Keep moving, man.

MAN: I paid my twenty-five cents. No one said I couldn't talk to the exhibits.

GUARD: You are talking to a lady, sir.

MAN: Lady! Hah! That's a piece of fancy business if I ever saw one. What's she doing showing herself off like that, eh? Letting people stare at her.

(MUSIC: Slides in as bridge to next scene.)

(Moving off.) Huh! Lady, my eye.

Scene Seven: Basement

(SOUND: Sleeping animals.)

ZIP: Here, my woolly wonder, here's a treat for you.

(SOUND: Horse eating sugar, an appreciative whinny.)

So, how was the first day out for the celebrated Canadian giantess?

ANNA: Awful.

ZIP: You're lucky. There're not nearly so many giants as dwarves. Only two other giantesses in the world that I've heard tell of … a German lady who died young, and a Russian, but she wasn't as tall as you.

ANNA: *(Hesitant.)* Really?

ZIP: Being a freak myself I make a study of curiosities—at least the living ones. Does he have you wearing false shoes?

ANNA: I won't do it.

ZIP: Ah well, you don't really need to. The public will love you anyway. *(To horse.)* Another lump of sugar, darling?

(SOUND: More feeding of horse.)

ANNA: I was thinking … perhaps some of us could do more than just exhibit. We could give lectures, help people understand …

ZIP: Lectures! Is that how they treat freaks where you come from?

ANNA: I don't know what you mean.

ZIP: I mean, do they have laws there to keep people from staring at you?

ANNA: Of course not. But it's my home.

ZIP: Would they like a black dwarf with a cone-shaped head?

ANNA: *(Hesitant.)* I don't know.

ZIP: I doubt it.

ANNA: I'm sure people would be … very kind.

(SOUND: The horse whinnies plaintively.)

ZIP: Don't look so sad, Miss Swan. It's only a poor dumb animal.

Scene Eight: The Letter

(SOUND: Gallery noise, distant yet harsh.)

MOTHER: Dear Anna,

Oh my dear daughter, how are you? We think of you so often in the city so far away. Mrs. Roy showed me a picture from a New York paper that had you in it. Wearing a very fine dress. We sure hope you are happy. I don't know what we would do without the money. It's been a very bad winter for your father's health. The boys are fine. God be with you.

Your loving mother, Sarah.

Scene Nine: Albinos' Room

(MUSIC: "Albino" theme, underneath.)

ANNA: *(Internal.)* For three weeks I endured exhibiting on my little podium, speaking to no one but Zip. Then one of the albino girls who room next to me asked if I would like to pay them a visit. I did not want to appear rude, so I agreed. The room was ill-lit and smelled strongly of mint and lavender. Lucia was lying down on a little settee in nothing but a light slip, and Alphonsia sat smoking a cigarette in the window.

(MUSIC: "Albino" theme out.)

LUCIA: Miss Swan, why don't you sit down?

ANNA: Thank you, I …

ALPHONSIA: We have made a special arrangement with the chairs.

(SOUND: Scrape of chair being adjusted.)

ANNA: *(Genuinely pleased.)* How kind of you.

LUCIA: You talk in your sleep, Miss Swan. We can hear you through the walls.

ANNA: Oh dear, I hope I don't disturb you.

LUCIA: *(Laughs.)* You are very entertaining. You talk a lot about a ta ta ma goose.

ALPHONSIA: *(Laughs.)* Is it a creature native to Nova Scotia?

ANNA: Tatamagouche! It's a town. I am homesick.

LUCIA: We'll cheer you up then. Do you believe in second sight?

ANNA: Perhaps …

LUCIA: Here, let's try a little experiment. Alphonsia, put on a blindfold.

(SOUND: ALPHONSIA giggles. The snap of a cloth.)

Now Miss Swan, if you will allow me to take an object from your bag.

(SOUND: Clasp opening.)

Sister, tell me *what* is this?

(MUSIC: Magical version of "Albino" theme.)

ALPHONSIA: A watch.

LUCIA: *Say* now what it is made of?

ALPHONSIA: Silver.

LUCIA: Can you tell me what this *might* be?

ALPHONSIA: A piece of money.

LUCIA: *Can* you tell me what it is made of?

ALPHONSIA: Copper.

ANNA: *(Internal, over the sisters' dialogue.)* How did she do it? I was amazed. They seemed to speak through a kind of telepathy.

LUCIA: I see we have caught your fancy.

ANNA: I am amazed. May I try asking a question myself?

(SOUND: Rustle of paper as ANNA draws a newspaper cutting from her purse; clasp shuts.)

LUCIA: I think we have done enough.

ANNA: But why?

LUCIA: She is tired.

ANNA: Just one more question. Alphonsia, what do I have in my hand?

(MUSIC: "Albino" theme out.)

LUCIA: *(After a pause.)* What have we—

ANNA: Don't say anything.

ALPHONSIA: A … ask me again—I cannot quite see it?

ANNA: What do I have in my hand?

ALPHONSIA: There are storm clouds. I cannot see clearly.

LUCIA: What have we *here* before us, sister?

(MUSIC: "Albino" theme seeps back.)

ANNA: I asked you not to say anything.

ALPHONSIA: A horse. I see a horse!

ANNA: What kind of horse?

(MUSIC: "Albino" theme out.)

(Pause.) What is it made of? *(Pause.)* All right, you ask her.

LUCIA: How is it *prepared* for us, dear sister?

(MUSIC: "Albino" theme returns, confidently.)

ALPHONSIA: Of paper. It is a horse made of paper.

ANNA: Yes, that's it, an advertisement from the newspaper for Barnum's Woolly Horse. "How is it prepared?" Why, it's all in the way you ask the question!

(SOUND: Peals of laughter from LUCIA and ALPHONSIA.)

So that is the secret of second sight.

LUCIA: You are quick, Miss Swan. Not many have guessed our secret. Will you have a drink with us?

ANNA: Thank you.

(MUSIC: "Albino" theme ends with a flourish.)

Scene Ten: Albinos' Room

(SOUND: Tinkling of glasses, drinks being poured.)

LUCIA: We are slow to make friends here. We rely on each other for amusement.

ANNA: You know Mr. Jackson?

LUCIA: No Mr. Jackson here.

ALPHONSIA: The dwarf, Lucia.

LUCIA: Zip! Why didn't you say so?

ANNA: He fools the public everyday, making them think he is an ape. What an amazing performance! And you two trick them with the "gift" of second sight. They don't see how clever you are. I stand there, day in, day out, just being gawked at. How I wish I could do something of value. As it is, I am no better than the poor dumb horse with sheep's wool stuck all over it.

ALPHONSIA: That's not true, Anna. You are a marvellous powerful woman. You remind me of, of … of … Fanny Kemble!

ANNA: *She* doesn't stand eight feet tall and weigh over four hundred pounds. I would never be taken seriously on the stage. *(Pause.)* Just as I was never really taken seriously at Teacher's College.

ALPHONSIA: We have never been taken seriously at all.

LUCIA: No one can ever tell us apart for one thing.

ANNA: That could be an advantage you know … or at least lead to all kinds of adventures … like Viola and Sebastian in *Twelfth Night*.

ALPHONSIA: Oh I love Shakespeare.

(MUSIC: "Shakespeare" theme starts underneath.)

ANNA: That's it! We could do a play! Just for the fun of it. We could stage *Twelfth Night*. You two can play Viola and Sebastian, the brother and sister who look so much alike they are always being confused and let's see … Of course Zip can play Malvolio, the unhappy steward. He is a very fine actor, I think, and that really is the best part. Now for Sir Toby and Sir Andrew …

ALPHONSIA: Chang and Eng, the Siamese Twins.

ANNA: Perfect … now what about …

LUCIA: Barnum will never let the freaks do plays.

ANNA: But if we rehearsed in secret and then presented it, he couldn't stop us, with the public there.

ALPHONSIA: Now that's not a bad idea.

LUCIA: It's dangerous, if Barnum suspected.

ANNA: He won't suspect. Not until it hits him over the head and then he'll see what freaks can do.

LUCIA: You have a mind as large as your body, Miss Swan …

(MUSIC: "Shakespeare" theme swells, then out.)

Scene Eleven: Basement

(SOUND: Scraping of chairs, soft animal sounds. Tittering and murmuring in background.)

ZIP: *(As Malvolio; nervous, flat.)* Were not you even now with the Countess Olivia?

ALPHONSIA: *(As Viola.)* Even now, sir. On a moderate pace I have since arrived but hither.

ZIP: *(As Malvolio.)* She returns this ring to you, sir. You might have saved me my pains to have taken it away yourself.

ALPHONSIA: *(As Viola.)* She took the ring of me. I'll none of it.

ANNA: *(Internal, over the acting.)* Alphonsia's got it, if only Zip weren't so nervous.

ZIP: *(As Malvolio.)* Come sir, you peevishly threw it to her, and her will is, it should be returned—

ANNA: *(Interrupting.)* That's fine, that's very good, but Zip—you could scorn her a little more. You seem so friendly.

ZIP: *(As Malvolio; with heavy scorn.)* Come sir, you peevishly threw it to her, and her will is, it should be returned.

ANNA: Good. But think about all those people staring at you so rudely in the cage. Think you are getting your revenge on them.

(MUSIC: Accompanies ZIP.)

ZIP: *(As Malvolio; completely true.)* If it be worth stooping for, there it lies, in your eye, if not, be it his that finds it.

ANNA: *(Internal, over.)* I had never had so much fun since I was a child. We met in the basement between the aquarium tank and the stables. I'll swear the animals came to enjoy our rehearsals for they would get quiet after a bit and just seemed to listen. *(Aloud.)* Excellent, excellent, excellent!

(SOUND: Laughter and approval from others.)

(Internal.) Madame Clofullia, the Bearded Lady, was to play Orsino, the Count.

CLOFULLIA: *(With a slight accent.)* It's not right, Anna. For years the public think I am a man. Sometimes they even come up and pull at my beard to see if Barnum stuck it on. If it weren't for the money—I would spit on them. I have a husband and two children. I am a woman. Now to play at being a man, isn't that wrong somehow, after all I've been through ...?

ANNA: No, no, no. Don't you see, Madame Clofullia? You are showing them your true spirit. You are in control now. It doesn't matter that you are a man or a woman, but that you are a breathing, loving, passionate person. What they saw as a deformity is transformed into beauty, and they will listen to you as they never have before.

(SOUND: Woolly horse whinnies.)

There, you see, he agrees with me. Now try it again.

(MUSIC: Accompanies CLOFULLIA.)

CLOFULLIA: *(As Orsino.)* Come hither boy.
If ever thou shalt love,

In the sweet pangs of it remember me,
For such as I am all true lovers are,
Unstaid and skittish in all motions else ...

ANNA: *(Internal, over.)* When I saw her next, on her little podium in the exhibition hall, she had such a look of nobility about her. Even the swags and fools who came to gawk showed a bit more respect.

CLOFULLIA: *(As Orsino.)* Save in the constant image of the creature
That is beloved.

(MUSIC: Out.)

ANNA: *(Internal.)* I had a little more trouble with Chang and Eng. Joined at the chest, but otherwise always at odds. Chang drinks, Eng is a teetotaller. As Alphonsia had warned me, they were full of trouble.

ENG: *(As Sir Andrew.)* No, faith, I'll not stay a jot longer.

CHANG: *(As Sir Toby.)* Thy reason, dear venom, give thy reason.

ENG: *(As Sir Andrew.)* Marry, I saw your niece do more favours to the Count's servingman than she ever bestowed upon me. I saw 't i' the orchard.

CHANG: Why don't you say "I saw it in the orchard"? That's what he's saying, isn't it? Not "I saw 't i' the orchard."

ENG: That, dear brother, is, however, the way it is written, in the text, if you had bothered to look at it ... the text.

CHANG: Don't start with me, you nose-picker.

ENG: Why you drunken, filthy ...

ANNA: Gentlemen, please, we are doing Shakespeare!

(MUSIC: Slides underneath.)

(Internal.) The plan was to have our first presentation in the gallery on the Twelfth Night of Christmas, true to the spirit of the play, and at a time when the museum would be generally quiet. Alphonsia and Lucia had been busy sending out invitations for a "startling new theatrical event" to a patrons list they had secured from a nearby theatre. Barnum was always talking about attracting a "better class of people to the museum." Well, this would do it for him, whether he liked it or not ...

(MUSIC: Out abruptly.)

Scene Twelve: Barnum's Office

(SOUND: Creaky swivel chair, muffled gallery.)

ANNA: You wanted to see me, Mr. Barnum?

BARNUM: You seem preoccupied of late, Anna. Sometimes when you exhibit, your mind seems not to be there at all. I've had some members of the public ask if you were a wax model. Now I'm not paying you good money to have them think that, am I?

ANNA: No sir, although I hear people pay a lot to see such things at Madame Tussaud's in London.

(SOUND: A match is struck.)

BARNUM: Yes well … *(Puffs on cigar.)* That's not quite the same thing, is it? Those were famous people, great villains or heroines, immortalized in wax. Here people pay to see living curiosities, live freaks.

ANNA: I will try and smile more, Mr. Barnum.

BARNUM: That's all I ask, and a few friendly words. Lord knows you speak well enough when you want to.

ANNA: Thank you.

BARNUM: And another thing. I've heard the strangest rumour that there is to be some sort of event held in the museum on the twelfth. I don't know if you know anything about that, but in any case, it's out of the question. I'm having the men pump out the whale tank that evening and there will be hoses running everywhere.

ANNA: But what about the whales?

BARNUM: The creatures are very sickly and not proving to be the attraction I had hoped.

ANNA: Are you just going to leave them to die!

(MUSIC: Anguished, sliding underneath.)

BARNUM: The carcasses will be sold for oil. I have some African elephants coming and they'll need the space.

ANNA: But it's so crowded down there, and overheated! The whales are sick because you should be using salt water, not fresh.

BARNUM: Are all Canadians such experts on whales? *(Moving off.)* In any case, the tanks will be drained that night, and there is nothing more to be said about it.

(SOUND: A heavy door opens.)

Good day.

(MUSIC: Out.)

(SOUND: Door shuts.)

Scene Thirteen: Basement

(SOUND: Slumbering horses, occasional slap of water from tank. Excited voices.)

ANNA: Chang! Eng! Madame Clofullia! There's still time to figure something out.

LUCIA: We can reach all the people we contacted. Tell them the performance has been cancelled.

CLOFULLIA: Why cancelled? Why not just postponed?

LUCIA: He'll be watching us from now on. There won't be another opportunity.

ZIP: What about finding another place? A hall somewhere?

ANNA: If we perform off the premises, then legally we've broken our contract with him. It says nothing about surprise performances "on the premises."

ALPHONSIA: We could talk to the men, ask them to come later.

CLOFULLIA: It's a terrible shame about the whales, poor creatures.

LUCIA: The men won't listen to freaks.

ANNA: Wait a minute! There's another way. We'll invite *more* people, not turn them away. We can run a giant advertisement in the New York Times on the day, so it's too late for Barnum to cancel. We'll make it a special show to raise money for the whales, to buy them proper tanks. Chang, you prepare the notes to the press.

ENG: Just don't get drunk.

CHANG: I never get drunk.

ANNA: Now you two stop it! We'll invite all of New York City. Charge five cents. Save the aquarium tank.

ALPHONSIA: Save the whales!

(MUSIC: Triumphant flourish.)

LUCIA: It has a certain ring to it.

(MUSIC: Triumphant flourish.)

(SOUND: Murmurs of approval, making of plans, etc.)

(MUSIC: Flourish grows hesitant, transforms into a wistful "Scots" theme.)

Scene Fourteen: The Second Letter

MOTHER: Dear Anna,

It's been so long since we heard from you, I fear you cannot be well. I have great news. Papa has found a job in the land claims office in New Glasgow. The money is very good and regular so we will be able to bring you home. I know it's been hard on you, Anna, but it's all over now. Harris will come to fetch you as soon as he can arrange it.

Love, Mother.

P.S. I shouldn't say anything yet, but I've heard there might be a job for a schoolteacher in New Glasgow. Oh Anna, wouldn't it be a marvel if they were to consider you?

ANNA: *(Internal.)* The play had so absorbed me, I had almost forgotten my homesickness. I couldn't think of telling my mother that I was obligated to Barnum for at least another year and a half. There were too many other things to worry about …

(MUSIC: "Scots" theme out.)

Scene Fifteen: Barnum's Gallery

(SOUND: Doors rattling, keeping out a great crowd of people. Rustling costumes, running steps back and forth. The "freaks" are inside preparing for the show: titters, nervous conversation, voice exercises.)

ALPHONSIA: A lot of people are going to have to stand. A lot of people aren't going to make it in at all!

ANNA: Alphonsia, go and get into costume.

(SOUND: Doors are flung open, the brief clamour of a crowd, off. The doors shut them out, heavy steps approaching, over.)

ZIP: Who are they?

ANNA: Barnum's men.

EDWARDS: We're here to pump out the tanks in the basement.

ZIP: They'll die a slow death if you drain the water out.

EDWARDS: Mr. Barnum's orders.

ZIP: But they are animals like us, they can feel.

JONES: Hey, I'm no animal.

(SOUND: JONES grabs ZIP.)

ZIP: Let go of me!

(SOUND: Struggles and whimpers.)

EDWARDS: *(Over.)* Leave the chimp alone! We've got a job to do here. Mr. Barnum will settle with him.

(SOUND: The doors open suddenly and a great crowd enters.)

JONES: *(Over.)* What's the big lady up to?! She's lettin' the crowd in—!

ALPHONSIA: *(Calling, off.)* Anna, Anna, wait! We're not ready!

ANNA: *(Over the din.)* Ladies and gentlemen! Please take whatever seating you can find as quickly as possible. Unfortunately, many of you will have to stand. What we offer you tonight is something quite different from the regular museum fare. Tonight we are going to stage one of Shakespeare's great plays of love and laughter with a cast of actors you are used to seeing in very different roles. At the intermission, we will pass the hat and ask that you all pay five cents, not for us, but to save the lives of the poor creatures downstairs. Fortunately, this performance stays their execution. And now, let the play begin.

(MUSIC: "Renaissance" theme, a simple lyre and lute, "With a hey, ho, the wind and the rain.")

CLOFULLIA: *(As Orsino.)* If music be the food of love, play on,
Give me excess of it, that, surfeiting,
The appetite may sicken and so die.

EDWARDS: *(Over.)* We can't empty the tanks with this crowd here.

JONES: Damn freaks are taking over the place.

LADY ONE: Shhh!

LADY TWO: I think they are very good.

(MUSIC: Sting: fear.)

(SOUND: Doors thrown open, one man's steps echo down the aisle, underneath.)

CLOFULLIA: *(As Orsino.)* O, when mine eyes did see Olivia first,
Methought she purged the air of pestilence!

EDWARDS and JONES: *(In unison, over.)* It's the boss!

BARNUM: What is going on here?

LADY ONE: Shhh!

LADY TWO: *(Hushed tones.)* A play, now quiet, or I'll have you put out.

BARNUM: *(Indignant.)* A play! By whom, madame, and at whose behest?

LADY TWO: Why Mr. Barnum's, of course. And a very humanitarian cause too, to save those poor whales. Anyone who interferes should be horsewhipped.

BARNUM: Madame, I—

LADY ONE: Shhh!

LADY TWO: And only charging five cents. I'm going to give him a dollar for all his trouble. I only wish more rich men had his sense of conscience.

ZIP: *(As Malvolio.)* She returns this ring to you, sir. You might have saved me my pains, to have taken it away yourself.

(MUSIC: "Renaissance" theme out.)

ANNA: *(Internal, over.)* We didn't know Barnum had been there until after the show when someone said they spotted him in the crowd. By then we were so happy as almost not to care.

(SOUND: Enthusiastic applause. Cries of "Bravo!" and "Save the whales!")

ALPHONSIA: Can you believe it? They loved us, they loved us, Anna.

ANNA: *(Laughing.)* "Love's night is noon," my sweet Cesario.

CHANG: My Sir Toby brought the house down.

ENG: You are drunk. It was *my* Sir Andrew.

ANNA: You were both wonderful!

ZIP: I have never felt so exhilarated!

ALPHONSIA: Listen, they are calling for us to take another bow.

(MUSIC: Starts to pound ominously.)

(SOUND: Applause turns to confusion, then panic. Cries of "Where are the doors?" "Get the ladies out," etc. Seats being pushed aside and fire far off in the distance.)

ANNA: What's that?

LUCIA: Something else is happening. I can hear Barnum.

BARNUM: *(Over the din.)* Please don't panic! I assure you, ladies and gentlemen, the fire department has been alerted and will be here as soon as possible. Our men will lead you to the exits, everyone will leave safely. Your money for tonight will be refunded.

(SOUND: Fire up, crowd clamouring, faint sounds of frightened menagerie begin.)

ANNA: What's he talking about?

(SOUND: Increased confusion, audience panicking and stampeding to the doors. Louder cries of distress from the animals. BARNUM trying to reassure crowd. Fire developing underneath.)

CLOFULLIA: *(Rushing in.)* There's fire in the basement, smoke everywhere!

ZIP: Someone has to get the animals loose!

ANNA: No, no, you can't go down there, you'll never get out ...!

EDWARDS: The floor's going!

(SOUND: The floor collapses. Screams.)

ZIP: They can't just leave them!

ANNA: Somebody stop him! Zip!

JONES: Watch out for the ceiling!

(SOUND: Part of the ceiling caves in. There are screams of panic, "Move aside," "Over there," "Help me," etc. Voices fade as the sound of the fire intensifies. Sound becomes a delirium echo, underneath.)

(MUSIC: Out.)

Scene Sixteen: Hospital Room

(SOUND: Rustle of skirts and hushed whispers, as in Scene One.)

NURSE: Miss Swan, Miss Swan, can you hear me?

ANNA: *(Internal.)* I can hear you.

NURSE: You have some friends to see you.

ANNA: *(Internal.)* Friends?

ALPHONSIA: Oh Anna, Anna, you're going to be all right. I know it.

ANNA: *(Haltingly.)* Alphonsia?

ALPHONSIA: Yes, darling, it's me and Lucia. Oh, you've been asleep for over a week!

LUCIA: They lowered you out the window over the heads of thousands of onlookers. It was quite a sight. *(A joke.)* If Barnum could have charged admission, I'm sure he would have.

ANNA: *(Still haltingly.)* Zip?

LUCIA: He died, Anna. With most of the animals. They found him in the stables.

NURSE: Now, now, don't let's upset her. She'll be back to normal in no time.

ANNA: Normal ... no, not normal.

ALPHONSIA: No one could stop him, Anna. There was nothing we could do.

(MUSIC: Swells, then settles underneath.)

Scene Seventeen: The Letter Home

(SOUND: Pen scratching.)

ANNA: Dear Mama,

In light of the recent tragic events, Mr. Barnum has agreed to breaking off the terms of my contract. In exchange for certain promises on our part, he has agreed to pay us off well.

I must tell you that I have given it a lot of thought and have decided not to return to New Annan. I will be leaving for Europe within the month. I will be travelling with Alphonsia and Lucia di Lugar, from Madagascar. We have become friends here and have worked out an act together, which we feel sure the public will find more entertaining than mere exhibiting.

Please tell my brothers and sisters that I think of them often. I enclose a cheque for their welfare. I know you will see it wisely spent.

Dear Mama, I do appreciate your offer to bring me home, but I think it is best I stay with this life to which I have become accustomed. In fact, I can say I have begun to take a certain pride in being one of the world's "greatest living curiosities."

Your loving daughter, Anna Swan.

(MUSIC: "With a hey, ho, the wind and the rain." The end.)

Compañeras

by

Carol Bolt

Compañeras was commissioned by the Canadian Broadcasting Corporation for Studio '93, and first broadcast on the CBC Stereo network on March 12, 1993, with the following cast:

Alison Sealy-Smith (Karen / Robo)
Alisa Palmer (Daysi)
Malika Mendez (Marcella)
Guillermo Verdecchia (Consul / Soldier Two)
Louis Di Bianco (Priest / Captain / Soldier Three)
Robert Persichini (Soldier One)

Produced and directed in Toronto by Baŋuta Rubess. Original music by Ramiro Puerta. Casting Consultant: Linda Grearson. Recording Engineer: John Marynowicz. Sound effects by Joe Hill. Production Assistant: Peggy Este. Script Editor: Ann Jansen. Executive Producer of Studio '93: Bill Lane.

Introduction

Five years after the events of Karen Ridd's story and four years after meeting her, I'm still inspired by what she did because it shows us change is possible. We can stand up for what we think is right. We can make a difference. It's a story that makes us all brave.

It's a wonderful story, so big with so many textures and colours, so hard to contain in a half-hour format, that I hope I can write about it again. The first draft of this play reached more than eighty pages. So much has been left out. Some of the scenes you didn't hear and won't read are:

The Story of Renaldo the Snake: When Karen is waiting to be questioned by the Treasury Police, refugees from the bombing wander in and out, visiting brothers and uncles and fathers, trailing household baggage. One shopping bag undulates. It is filled with Renaldo, a pet snake, and work stops while the young soldiers find an excuse to visit this marvel.

The Story of Marcella's Birthday Party: While Marcella celebrates her birthday, soldiers storm the Peace Brigades house, running over the roof, appearing at grilled windows, all wearing wool ski-masks in spite of the heat. They tear the house apart looking for subversive material, but they miss the revolutionary poster because it's on the back of the bathroom door. Karen is ill with fever. Everything seems surreal. The young soldiers are charmed by the young Peace Brigades workers. They take off their ski-masks. They eat cake, no longer terrible. They agree they will come back for tea one day.

The Story of the Fourth Woman: Daysi. Marcella. Karen. There is another woman in the story, arrested with Karen and Marcella, who did not walk back into the prison, as Karen did. It would be interesting to explore her choice as well as Karen's.

The Stories of Peace Brigades: Working for Peace Brigades means starting cars which may be car bombed, answering doors for people whose lives have been threatened, standing watch all night in the union office of a newspaper because a bomb threat has been received. Peace Brigades work is filled with choices that make a difference. Karen stopped a kidnapping in progress at a demonstration simply by taking pictures of it.

The Stories of the People of El Salvador: Karen would tell you the story is not about her. It's about the people of El Salvador. Their struggle inspired everything she did and theirs is the real story.

The Stories of Robo the Clown: I am pleased to introduce you to Karen's clown, Robo, but I have not done him justice. Robo is actually a mute clown, but the challenge involved in radio mime was overwhelming.

CAROL BOLT

Characters

KAREN: Karen Ridd

ROBO: Karen Ridd's clown and alter ego

DAYSI:A Salvadoran working for The Union of the Unemployed

MARCELLA: A Peace Brigades worker from Columbia

SOLDIER ONE, SOLDIER TWO and SOLDIER THREE

PRIEST and CONGREGATION

CAPTAIN

CONSUL

Compañeras

Scene One: Hospital

(MUSIC: "Clown" theme.)

(SOUND: Hospital ambience, up and continuing underneath.)

KAREN: *(Internal.)* It happened this way. A young woman from Winnipeg, Manitoba, was working as a clown …

(SOUND: Clown noises, honks and whistles.)

(Internal.) She made video tapes for a hospital, to help children deal with treatments that they didn't understand …

ROBO: Mechana …

KAREN: Don't worry, Robo …

ROBO: Mechana. Gros mechana. Nix mechana. *["Big machine. No way."]*

(SOUND: Bells and whistles indicate ROBO is worried; they continue underneath.)

KAREN: It's just a machine that takes pictures of your head.

ROBO: Nix mein kopla. *["Not my head."]*

KAREN: Please don't worry, Robo. It doesn't hurt and it can't tell what you're thinking.

ROBO: Rayvee? *["Really?"]*

KAREN: Look at it, Robo. If you see what it is, it won't scare you.

ROBO: Rayvee?

KAREN: Electroencephalograph.

ROBO: *(Discovers.)* Selectoandparamet …

KAREN: Sure. That's close, Robo. Watch, see, I just put this on my head. It's like a hat.

ROBO: *(With enthusiastic noise-making.)* Kopla topper ha ha ya ya. *["Robo wants the hat. It's funny."]*

KAREN: *(Internal, over.)* My name is Karen Ridd. Robo is my alter ego. He is not a very smart clown, he's not a very brave clown, but clowns are anarchists, they're order-breakers, so in 1988, having taped his reactions to EEG's and fracture clinics, Robo and I decided on a new career …

Scene Two: Interior Dialogue

(SOUND: Enthusiastic bells and whistles, underneath.)

KAREN: That's right, Robo …

ROBO: Ha ha kopla topper. Mucho grosso kopla topper. *["Robo's new career is making bigger funny hats."]*

KAREN: Robo and I decided to go to El Salvador …

(MUSIC: Synthesized brakes applied heavily.)

ROBO: Robo kay? *["Robo who?"]*

KAREN: Because Robo and I are clowns from Winnipeg, of course …

ROBO: El-sal-va-kay?

KAREN: We were raised in the United Church, the NDP. We grew up thinking it was possible to change the world …

ROBO: El-sal-va-far. El-sal-va-nix.

(SOUND: Horns and whistles as ROBO tries to get KAREN's attention, underneath.)

KAREN: Robo and I have a strong sense of right and wrong, an even stronger suspicion that absolutes are dangerous …

ROBO: Resta minim … *["Wait a minute …"]*

KAREN: Don't worry, Robo …

ROBO: El Sal-va …

(SOUND: ROBO begins a two-tone European siren noise, "Ee ah, ee ah …", which continues underneath.)

KAREN: It will be all right. Remember, clowns are healers.

ROBO: *(Stops his siren imitation.)* Ee ah … Rayvee?

KAREN: Laughing is healing. Remember that it's the court jester who heals the king's mind.

ROBO: Rayvee? Caramba!

(MUSIC: "El Salvador" theme.)

Scene Three: Office of The Union of the Unemployed

(SOUND: Phones, typewriters and the bustle of an office continue underneath.)

ROBO: *(Approaching a new language with energy and enthusiasm.)* Buenos dias ... Buenos dias ... Buenos dias ...

MARCELLA: Buenos dias, Karen.

KAREN: *(In good Anglo Spanish.)* Buenos dias.

DAYSI: Does your friend realise, Marcella, it's the third time she's said "buenos dias," this morning. To me, I mean.

MARCELLA: Or perhaps the fourth time.

DAYSI: Please tell her she's amiable.

KAREN: Muchas gracias.

ROBO: *(Enjoying the language, underneath the others, with reverb.)* Muchas gracias, muchas gracias ...

DAYSI: You and Marcella, you're both so polite. Is it because you're from the Peace Brigades?

KAREN: I'm sorry, I ...

ROBO: Habla inglés?

DAYSI: Peace. Brigades. International. It's a strange concept, don't you think?

KAREN: A strange what?

ROBO: *(With a little reverb.)* A strange kay?

DAYSI: Why is it you're here, Marcella?

MARCELLA: You know why.

DAYSI: Marcella has come all the way from Colombia and you have come from Canada. All to ensure that the police do not raid and the rhinoceros do not go on stampede.

ROBO: *(Savouring the Spanish.)* El rinoceronte.

KAREN: I'm sorry, my Spanish ...

DAYSI: The Union of the Unemployed receives a bomb threat, so Peace Brigades sends in a witness. Because then, of course, if there is a bomb, it blows up a tall blonde gringa, and it makes the North American newspapers and the government looks bad and the people who support the government look bad …

KAREN: I don't understand …

ROBO: *(Loves the strange word.)* El rinoceronte!

DAYSI: And you are successful, please don't think I'm not grateful … there are no bombs, it's as if bombs did not exist, and there are no rhinoceros and of course it is so much easier to work when the rhinoceros are not stampeding. Am I speaking too fast for you?

MARCELLA: Yes, Daysi, and you know you are.

DAYSI: She doesn't have the words, your friend. I mean in Spanish. The situation is surreal, is it not? Do you appreciate the surreality?

KAREN: I'm sorry, I …

DAYSI: El Salvador. My country. You'll grow to love it if you spend much time here. Tell her, Marcella. You've been here six months now.

MARCELLA: *(With a Spanish accent.)* Daysi's teasing you, Karen.

DAYSI: It is unbelievable. Nothing is believable, which gives everything a kind of magic, I suppose.

KAREN: Marcella, please tell her. If she could just speak more …

DAYSI: I live in a country where it seems it is necessary I'm protected from my countrymen. Because I want to do my job. I want to work here at The Union of the Unemployed. That is not a political act. I know, since I am not political. And usually, it is not an impossible act but there are days when a tall, fair, stranger saviour stands blocking my file drawer. Will you ask her to move, Marcella …

KAREN: I'm sorry …

(SOUND: File drawer opens, papers rustle underneath.)

DAYSI: A tall, fair, uncomprehending stranger saviour. But polite.

(SOUND: File drawer slams shut.)

KAREN: I'm sorry, I …

DAYSI: Do you understand one-fifth of what I'm saying?

ROBO: *(Savouring.)* El Salvador.

KAREN: I know I'm not supposed to be your saviour.

DAYSI: Your Spanish must be better than your accent.

KAREN: I hope so.

MARCELLA: If I may present Daysi Alonzo …

DAYSI: Tell her we are more alike than I admit, Marcella. Tell her I like her shoes.

Scene Four: Market

(MUSIC: Lively band blaring on the radio.)

(SOUND: Street market ambience, continues underneath.)

DAYSI: Do you like these shoes?

KAREN: Of course.

ROBO: Gustarle? Zapatos?

DAYSI: Do you think I should buy them? Red shoes? I'll wear red shoes and you'll wear your pants with the orange dots and purple lozenges. We will both make a statement.

KAREN: Statement?

ROBO: Zapatos rojos?

DAYSI: Don't worry, it's not a political statement. For me a fashion statement will suffice.

KAREN: Will what?

DAYSI: As I told you, I am not political.

KAREN: *(Quoting the song "A Bicycle Built for Two.")* "Daisy, Daisy …"

ROBO: *(Singing to the same tune.)* Mar-gar-ita.

DAYSI: Wear high heels. And pink. And smile a lot. We are women, we are not taken seriously. We must make macho work, or be clowns, don't you think?

ROBO: Pensar? Pensar?

KAREN: I don't believe you.

DAYSI: Why don't you buy shoes like this, Karen? So we can go dancing?

KAREN: I don't believe you could ever stand back and wear high heels and not speak out …

(SOUND: ROBO blows a high-pitched whistle.)

I don't believe that you don't care. Daysi, I'm serious …

DAYSI: Of course, since that's why you're here. Because things are serious.

KAREN: Do you have to make fun of me? All the time?

DAYSI: Karen, why don't you buy shoes like this? And I'll take you to La Puerta del Diablo.

Scene Five: La Puerta Del Diablo

(MUSIC: "La Puerta" theme, eerie and haunting.)

(SOUND: Wind underneath.)

ROBO: La Puerta del Diablo.

DAYSI: The Devil's Gate. My father tells stories of coming here for picnics as a child. But when I was a child it was much used as a body dump.

KAREN: I know.

DAYSI: It's beautiful, isn't it?

KAREN: I know about La Puerta del Diablo.

DAYSI: You can see for miles. You can see right over the city, except for the smog. Or would you call it mist?

KAREN: Daysi …

(SOUND: ROBO makes his European siren sound, which continues underneath.)

DAYSI: Mist sounds more magical, I think. And mist means you can't see the bodies, of course …

KAREN: You keep saying that you're not political.

DAYSI: Mist. It's all you see, but the city is still there, of course. And you can't see the bodies, but the places where the bodies were … they're still there, of course. Remembering the bodies, it's not a political act. It's a human act, isn't it? To forget the bodies, that would be political.

KAREN: I'm sorry, my Spanish …

DAYSI: I think El Salvador is like your movie.

KAREN: My what?

ROBO: Si. Muy cine.

DAYSI: And you are the hero in this movie …

KAREN: I'm what?

ROBO: Ser héroe.

DAYSI: But you're the tallest, the blondest, you save me from bomb threats. What did you do before you decided to save me from bomb threats?

(SOUND: KAREN laughs.)

Why are you laughing? Karen?

Scene Six: Visa Office

(SOUND: A hot office, one typewriter clicks along slowly, a fly buzzes around. A rubber stamp.)

SOLDIER ONE: You are Miss Karen Ridd … you are Canadian … and you wish to obtain an extension to a tourist visa …

KAREN: Yes, sir.

SOLDIER ONE: Might I ask why, Miss Ridd?

KAREN: I beg your pardon?

ROBO: Por que? A que discutir?

SOLDIER ONE: Are you working here in El Salvador, Miss Ridd?

KAREN: I'm sorry, my Spanish …

SOLDIER ONE: I ask you if you are employed.

ROBO: Empleo … empleado por …

KAREN: I'm trying to learn Spanish …

SOLDIER ONE: And if you were employed, what is it you would do, Miss Ridd?

KAREN: I'm sorry?

SOLDIER ONE: Your occupation? Your profession? When you are not a tourist, learning Spanish.

KAREN: I'm a clown.

(SOUND: ROBO laughs.)

SOLDIER ONE: I beg your pardon?

(SOUND: ROBO laughs.)

(SOUND: Goofy, synthesized sound as time passes.)

Scene Seven: Visa Office, Later

(SOUND: A balloon blowing up; it pops. A burst of male laughter, underneath.)

SOLDIER ONE: Señorita, Karen …

ROBO: El balon rinoceronte.

SOLDIER TWO: Señorita Karen, my balloon has broken … if I could have another …

SOLDIER ONE: With my balloons, I've made a beagle.

ROBO: El sabueso.

SOLDIER ONE: Señorita, my beagle … do you like him?

(SOUND: A balloon pops.)

SOLDIER TWO: Señorita?

SOLDIER ONE: You see, I've made him glasses. Little cardboard glasses just like mine.

SOLDIER TWO: Señorita? Another balloon por favor?

(SOUND: ROBO laughs.)

(SOUND: Goofy, synthesized sound fades.)

Scene Eight: Street

(MUSIC: Menacing band plays on the radio.)

(SOUND: Street ambience. A distant siren starts subliminally and slowly grows louder, underneath.)

DAYSI: Balloons! This scene will not be in your movie, I assure you.

ROBO: El perrito?

KAREN: *(Amused.)* They extended my visa.

ROBO: El rinoceronte.

DAYSI: We're not used to heroes carrying balloons, blowing up balloons, making sculptures of balloons.

ROBO: Ser héroe.

KAREN: I don't want to be a hero.

ROBO: Como no?

SOLDIER ONE: Excuse me, señorita …

SOLDIER TWO: We must ask for your identification, señorita.

KAREN: My name is Karen Ridd.

ROBO: Ser héroe.

SOLDIER TWO: Not you, señorita.

SOLDIER ONE: You are free to go.

KAREN: We have done nothing wrong. We are both free to go.

SOLDIER ONE: Your friend will come with us.

SOLDIER TWO: To answer questions.

KAREN: Do you think so?

DAYSI: Karen …

KAREN: I don't think so. I think I will stay. To take pictures. Do you mind if I take pictures?

ROBO: Sitzen photo. Ya. Ya.

(SOUND: Camera equipment being taken out.)

DAYSI: Karen, please …

KAREN: Smile Daysi … say "Cheese." … No, I don't think that's what you say in Spanish …

ROBO: Sitzen ha ha. Dicta fromagio.

(SOUND: Enthusiastic clown noisemakers, fading underneath.)

Scene Nine: Office of The Union of the Unemployed

(SOUND: An office clock ticks, a typewriter stops. KAREN blows her nose to finish a good cry.)

MARCELLA: *(With a Spanish accent.)* She's all right, Karen.

ROBO: Olé Robo! Bravo bravo Robo!

MARCELLA: *(Spanish accent.)* They questioned her, that's all.

KAREN: Was it my fault, Marcella?

MARCELLA: *(Spanish accent.)* No, of course not!

ROBO: Supra Robo!

KAREN: But why Daysi?

MARCELLA: Karen …

KAREN: Because Daysi's not political. Except that she knows me …

MARCELLA: *(Spanish accent, fading underneath.)* Karen, Daysi is political … everyone's political.

Scene Ten: Interior Monologue

(MUSIC: "Clown" theme, in a surreal prison, continues underneath.)

KAREN: *(Internal.)* Ten days later, Daysi disappeared. We had no trace of her, except for one red shoe that was left in the street. It was thirty-six hours until we heard she was alive, held in the women's prison.

(SOUND: Distorted hubbub of the prison courtyard. Shrieks and laughter. Women's voices in Spanish, lots of swearing; continuing underneath.)

(Internal.) The women's prison was a mad house.

ROBO: Señorita …

KAREN: *(Internal.)* The mad can be clowns. Six hundred years ago there were mad clowns. *Buffon*. The wounded, the lepers, dwarves, who tiptoed round as if their feet were pretty …

ROBO: Señorita … You're so tall and fair …

KAREN: *(Internal.)* They tiptoe around, full of compliments, but there's nothing but hate in their eyes.

ROBO: Can I help you, señorita?

KAREN: *(Internal.)* I'm looking for Daysi Alonzo.

(SOUND: ROBO shrieks with laughter.)

(Internal.) Gloria Daysi Alonzo Jaimes.

ROBO: *(Babbling.)* I am Daysi. I am she. I'm your friend, I'm your sister. What did you bring me? Are you taking me home, dear heart? Am I going home? *(Babbling continues underneath.)*

KAREN: *(Internal.)* Daysi saw me from across the courtyard.

(SOUND: Prison ambience no longer distorted, but crisp and real.)

(MUSIC: "Clown" theme out.)

ROBO: *(Babbling.)* Karen? Is that your name? Karen? My sister, my friend, my compañera? Karen? Do you have food? Are you taking me home? Karen, compañera? *(Babbling continues underneath.)*

KAREN: *(Internal.)* Daysi ran toward me, but before she took more than three steps, she fell. She couldn't get up. She'd been beaten, tortured. The young soldiers who questioned her had taken it in turns, to rape her, or kick her repeatedly in the spine.

DAYSI: I'm fine, Karen.

KAREN: Oh, Daysi …

DAYSI: I will be fine. I promise.

KAREN: Lean on me. Let me help.

DAYSI: The woman you were talking to … did you help her?

(SOUND: Distant crazy laughter from ROBO.)

KAREN: Let me help you.

DAYSI: First they raped her. Vaginally. Then the commandant raped her anally and when he was done, he wiped his penis on her shirt.

ROBO: *(Laughing and babbling, underneath.)* Ha ha Robo. Ha ha, señor, muy bravo …

(MUSIC: "Clown" theme, disturbed, creeps back.)

KAREN: I am a clown.

(MUSIC: A clown explosion: the sound a clown makes when things are going very badly.)

I am Robo, the clown who is proud of his manicure until he discovers that he has no hands.

(SOUND: A real explosion.)

Clowns want to be loved. That may be all they want. And they are loved so they tend to think that things are simple.

(MUSIC: Barrel organ clown music cranked erratically, underneath.)

Now I felt as if I had no hands. I felt as if I were no help. Daysi was in prison. El Salvador was changing. It had been a police state.

(SOUND: A siren begins to rise and fall, underneath.)

It was now a state at war with its civilian population. There was a shoot-on-sight curfew, more raids, more disappearances …

Scene Eleven: Prison

(SOUND: Prison courtyard ambience, continues underneath.)

ROBO: *(Singing lustily to the tune of "A Bicycle Built for Two.")* Mar-gar-it-a. Esta peligrosa. No tengo miedo …

KAREN: Daysi, she won't let go of you.

DAYSI: I think it's because I taught her your song.

ROBO: *(Singing.)* No tengo miedo.

DAYSI: She takes it as a sign of friendship.

ROBO: *(Singing.)* All for the love of you …

DAYSI: She doesn't understand I'm leaving, do you, compañera?

ROBO: *(Singing.)* Daisy, Daisy …

DAYSI: You can help me say good-bye, Karen. You can give her a present …

ROBO: *(Singing.)* Daisy, Daisy …

DAYSI: You can blow up one of your balloons. You can make her a bird or a monkey … you'd like that, compañera, would you not?

ROBO: I'm half crazy …

DAYSI: Everybody likes balloons.

KAREN: Daysi …

ROBO: Daisy, Daisy …

DAYSI: But hurry, Karen, or we'll miss the bus. And I won't get back to work this afternoon.

KAREN: You aren't going back to work today.

DAYSI: Of course I am.

KAREN: That's crazy, Daysi …

DAYSI: No, it's simple. If I don't go, then it means they've won. And they haven't won. They can't think that they've won.

KAREN: Daysi, forget it. Please, you're not political, remember.

DAYSI: But Karen, to not work against them. I think that would be political.

KAREN: *(Internal.)* So we went back to work. We all went back to work. Six weeks later, the university was attacked again.

Scene Twelve: Church

(MUSIC: A sombre drum introduces the church service.)

(SOUND: A microphone squeaks in a cavernous room, murmuring of the congregation, shuffling feet.)

PRIEST: We are gathered with our martyrs. Father Ignacio Martin Baro.

CONGREGATION: Presente.

PRIEST: Father Segundo Montes.

CONGREGATION: Presente.

PRIEST: Father Ignacio Ellacuria.

CONGREGATION: Presente.

PRIEST: Father Amado Lopez.

CONGREGATION: Presente.

PRIEST: Father Juan Ronon Moreno.

CONGREGATION: Presente.

PRIEST: Father Joaquin Lopez y Lopez.

CONGREGATION: Presente.

PRIEST: Elba Julia Ramos.

CONGREGATION: Presente.

KAREN: *(Internal, over.)* Six Jesuit priests, their housekeeper and her daughter were murdered. In El Salvador a memorial service takes a certain form. The martyrs' names are read and the congregation responds "Presente."

(SOUND: The roll call of names and the response, "Presente," continues.)

(Internal.) It's a simple and beautiful statement, and of course, it's dangerous. You know you are in the company of the martyrs. You know you may join them.

Scene Thirteen: Church Sanctuary, Dawn

(SOUND: Birds chirp outside. People sleeping. Loud knocking on huge church door, people waking up, disoriented, Spanish dialogue.)

KAREN: *(Internal.)* The air force had begun a bombing campaign against its own civilians. Marcella and I were assigned to the Lutheran church, assisting refugees.

(SOUND: Louder knocking.)

SOLDIER TWO: *(Through a distant loudspeaker.)* Es la policía.

KAREN: *(Internal.)* Five hundred refugees at the church, seeking sanctuary.

(SOUND: A baby cries.)

MARCELLA: Karen … Karen … wake up?

ROBO: Nononono …

KAREN: What time is it?

ROBO: Nononono …

MARCELLA: It's five a.m. Get dressed okay?

(SOUND: Breaking glass.)

ROBO: *(Like a siren, frightened.)* Nononono ...

MARCELLA: The police are here. And you can't get arrested in that T-shirt. Please, Karen. It says "Liberation Theology."

Scene Fourteen: Truck

(SOUND: Truck driving over rough terrain, underneath.)

KAREN: *(Internal.)* We were handcuffed, blindfolded. We were thrown in the back of a truck.

SOLDIER ONE: Do you know where you're going, girls?

SOLDIER TWO: La Puerta del Diablo.

(MUSIC: The eerie theme of "La Puerta" creeps in.)

ROBO: La Puerta del Diablo.

SOLDIER ONE: La Puerta del Diablo. Have you seen the view?

(SOUND: SOLDIERS laugh, underneath.)

ROBO: *(Babbling underneath.)* La-puerta-del-diablo-la-puerta-del-diablo-la-puerta-del ...

MARCELLA: *(Whispers.)* Karen? It's all right. We'll stay together. For as long as we can.

ROBO: *(Moans.)* No no no no noo noo noo ...

MARCELLA: We'll stay together. We'll leave together. We'll walk out together. From wherever it is that they take us.

ROBO: No hablo español.

KAREN: We'll stay together. Because we're compañeras.

(SOUND: The truck motor grows louder, drowning out nearly all other sound.)

(Internal.) At Peace Brigades, we'd discussed what we'd do when picked up by police. Survival strategy. And I'd decided I would answer all their questions in as much detail as possible. The clown who says too much.

(MUSIC: "Clown" theme, very slow and stealthy.)

Scene Fifteen: Interrogation Room

(SOUND: A cigar is lit. A clock ticks.)

CAPTAIN: Your name is Karen Ridd.

KAREN: Karen Elizabeth Ridd. *(Spelling her name.)* K. A. R. E. N. E. L. I. Z. A. B. E. T. H. R. I. D. D. I was named for my father's grandmother. *(Internal.)* I would provide much too much information. I would look at every question metaphysically.

CAPTAIN: Perhaps you will tell us what you're doing in El Salvador …

KAREN: It happened this way … I know it sounds unlikely, but I was working as a clown. At a hospital. In Winnipeg. In Canada. With kids. I was Robo the clown.

ROBO: El-sal-va- *(Siren effect, continuing underneath.)*

CAPTAIN: My question is why are you here. In El Salvador. Today.

KAREN: I'm trying to explain.

CAPTAIN: No, señorita, you are trying to fill in time. You're trying to entertain me.

KAREN: I'm sorry, my Spanish … *(Apologizing continues.)*

(Internal, over her apologizing.) As survival strategy, the technique may be transparent but this doesn't mean it's not effective. The storyteller can control the story and the prisoner who maintains control is not truly and totally a prisoner.

CAPTAIN: I'm not so sure this information is important, señorita.

KAREN: *(Internal.)* The object is to tell these stories well, so the listener will allow them to continue.

ROBO: Winnipeg. W. I. N. N. …

CAPTAIN: Señorita …

KAREN: *(Internal.)* Scheherazade. A woman, not a threat.

ROBO: Volleyball. V. O. L. L. …

CAPTAIN: I'm not so sure we need to know so much. About volleyball. About Winnipeg.

KAREN: *(Internal.)* A strange thing you should know. I wasn't afraid.

ROBO: Tengo miedo.

KAREN: No, Robo … not really afraid. Not because I was brave but because there wasn't time. I wasn't afraid. I wasn't alone. There was too much to think about. So many stories to tell. So many questions to answer.

CAPTAIN: *(Angry.)* We need to know your contacts in El Salvador. We need names of the people you work with.

KAREN: *(Internal.)* I knew that I'd be safer than Marcella. Because I'm tall and blond and she's small and dark. Because I'm North American and she's from Colombia.

(SOUND: Paper ripped in half.)

(SOUND: ROBO gasps.)

KAREN: *(Internal.)* I was safer. I was not immune.

CAPTAIN: The prisoner's statement is ingenuous.

KAREN: Is what?

ROBO: Ingenuo. Candoroso.

CAPTAIN: Do you think I'm naïve?

KAREN: I'm sorry, my Spanish is imperfect.

ROBO: Esta candoroso.

CAPTAIN: You're in El Salvador to work with subversives, señorita, the FMLN …

KAREN: I'm in El Salvador to learn about the country, because I find it beautiful. I'm working for …

CAPTAIN: We know who you're working for.

KAREN: I am working for Peace Brigades Inter—

(SOUND: A slap. KAREN cries out.)

Peace Brigades International which is non-violent, non-aligned—

(SOUND: More slaps: one, two. KAREN gasps and cries out.)

KAREN: *(Internal.)* Three hours of questions. And I am not beaten much …

CAPTAIN: I am frustrated, señorita, I'm afraid …

ROBO: *(Underneath.)* No tengo miedo, no tengo miedo.

CAPTAIN: It seems you've said so much yet you've told me so little.

(MUSIC: Stealthy "Clown" theme fades in.)

KAREN: *(Internal.)* Five hours of questions. I am Scheherazade …

ROBO: Ich bin ein Berliner, ein Winnipeger …

CAPTAIN: My clerk begs your indulgence. Since he must write down everything you say.

KAREN: *(Internal.)* Six hours of questions. So many stories I can't tell. Survival strategy. I take to asking questions of my own.

CAPTAIN: You are trying to entertain me, señorita.

KAREN: Do you have a family?

ROBO: Am I like your daughter? Like your sister?

KAREN: *(Internal.)* I have an agenda. Survival strategy. I have something I can do so I am not afraid. I have something I can do. I still have power.

CAPTAIN: I have a daughter. She is eight years old. This week.

ROBO: I am eight years old this week.

KAREN: *(Internal.)* And I am so much safer than so many. Because I'm tall. And blond. And North American …

CAPTAIN: But I regret, señorita, we have no more time for pleasantries.

(MUSIC: "Clown" theme pulls short, alarmed.)

KAREN: We don't?

ROBO: Como no?

CAPTAIN: It seems your consul has arrived. To secure your release.

Scene Sixteen: Prison Hallway

(SOUND: Military escort marching, keys jangling, prisoners' muffled curses and sobs, all underneath.)

KAREN: *(Internal.)* On the way out of the cell block, I saw Marcella. She was handcuffed, blindfolded, pushed face against the wall. Objectified. She wasn't a person. She was a prisoner. The image of a prisoner, nameless, faceless, forgotten … I knew I couldn't leave her as if she were a poster, ignored on a wall.

Scene Seventeen: Prison Office

(SOUND: Rubber stamp, pesky fly buzzes.)

SOLDIER ONE: Her name is Karen Ridd?

CONSUL: That's right.

SOLDIER ONE: Her papers seem to be in order.

CONSUL: Thank you.

SOLDIER ONE: And she's released to your authority.

CONSUL: Yes.

KAREN: No.

SOLDIER ONE: I beg your pardon?

CONSUL: He's saying you're released to my authority. Because I'm your consul.

KAREN: I know that.

CONSUL: He's saying you're free.

KAREN: I can't leave.

SOLDIER ONE: *(With a Spanish accent.)* Excuse me, señorita, but …

KAREN: I can't leave without my friend.

CONSUL: Of course you can.

KAREN: I'm sorry.

CONSUL: You realize, of course, that we've gone to some trouble to ensure your release, Miss Ridd.

(MUSIC: "Colombian" theme, with a driving rhythm, begins underneath.)

KAREN: I'm sorry.

CONSUL: You realize, of course, it's twenty minutes until curfew.

SOLDIER ONE: You realize, of course, your friend has been released.

KAREN: No, I'm sorry. She hasn't.

CONSUL: Miss Ridd …

KAREN: I've seen her.

CONSUL: Miss Ridd, we have to leave before the curfew.

KAREN: I'm sorry.

CONSUL: Your friend will have to work with her own consul.

KAREN: My friend is handcuffed, blindfolded. She's alone and I can't leave her. *(Internal.)* It wasn't brave. I didn't feel brave, it wasn't hard to say I couldn't leave. It seemed the only thing to say, it seemed right, of course, and also, to be honest, I didn't think they'd let me stay.

CONSUL: Miss Ridd, I must warn you …

KAREN: *(Internal.)* I imagined the scene in the movie. The heroine protests the hero's fate.

CONSUL: You're being very foolish.

KAREN: *(Internal.)* She throws herself in front of the firing squad, she's dragged away …

(SOUND: Briefcase snapped shut, chair pushed away.)

CONSUL: I can't help you, Miss Ridd.

KAREN: Please …

CONSUL: I can't order you to come with me.

KAREN: But you do understand, don't you?

CONSUL: No, I don't.

KAREN: You understand loyalty. And camaraderie. You understand, Marcella and I … we're compañeras.

CONSUL: I can guarantee your security now. If you come with me now.

KAREN: No. I can't.

(MUSIC: "Colombian" theme ends with a flourish.)

(SOUND: A rubber stamp.)

SOLDIER ONE: You will get what you want. We can give you what you want … if you choose to be in prison …

Scene Eighteen: Prison

(SOUND: Rattling bars. Hoots and jeers of young soldiers, "La quiero!" "Hey, gringa," air kisses, etc., underneath.)

ROBO: *(Talking back, underneath.)* Cojones grandes. La boca grande …

MARCELLA: *(Calling out.)* Karen!

(SOUND: Handcuffs being unlocked, soldiers saunter by.)

KAREN: *(Internal.)* They put us in a room together. I was blindfolded again, but they took Marcella's handcuffs off and we joined hands. The young soldiers came by the room where we'd been put. To see the curiosity.

SOLDIER ONE: Are these the girls who like us so much?

ROBO: Mucho macho!

SOLDIER TWO: Are you going to spend the night, girls?

SOLDIER ONE: They're holding hands.

ROBO: Macho mucho!

SOLDIER TWO: Do they like us? Or do they like each other?

(SOUND: SOLDIER TWO laughs, but his laugh peters out.)

(MUSIC: "Magic" theme, continuing underneath.)

KAREN: *(Internal.)* This is the magic. The soldiers became clowns. They wanted simple answers, or they wanted to be loved, perhaps, but something happened. Something changed. Something reached them.

SOLDIER TWO: Las putas … Las huecas …

SOLDIER ONE: Leave them alone.

SOLDIER THREE: *(With a Spanish accent.)* Si, deja las. Leave them alone. They're compañeras.

(MUSIC: A sweet crescendo, mingling of "Clown" and "El Salvador" themes, up and into next scene.)

Scene Nineteen: Interior Monologue

(SOUND: Siren and TV babble.)

KAREN: *(Internal.)* We were released at nine o'clock that evening. A military escort took us through the curfew. We went to the Hilton hotel where we watched CNN.

(SOUND: A clown explosion.)

ROBO: Esta Robo brava con El Sal-va … *(Makes explosion sound.)*

(SOUND: A real bomb drops in the distance.)

KAREN: *(Internal.)* We laughed a lot. We were clown CNN reporters as the news denied bombing we saw from our balcony.

ROBO: El *(Explosion sound.)* Esta de ningun manera una explosíon.

(SOUND: TV and siren out. Roll call of martyrs begins and continues underneath.)

KAREN: *(Internal.)* I wanted to tell Daysi what had happened. How simple it had seemed to know what to do, both for me and for the soldiers who recaptured me.

ROBO: *(Singing to the tune of "A Bicycle Built for Two," underneath.)* Mar-gar-ita … No tengas miedo …

KAREN: *(Internal.)* But we were asked to leave the country the next day. I came back to Canada, to write and talk about El Salvador … Marcella went to Mexico. Where she works with a union.

(SOUND: Roll call of martyrs continuing underneath.)

(Internal.) Daysi "disappeared" in December 1989. Her body was discovered six days later. She had been tortured for some time before she died. Daysi Alonzo Jaimes. Presente.

(SOUND: Sirens wail, then stop.)

(MUSIC: Big drum goes on for a long time. The end.)

Calamity Jane
AND THE FAT BUFFALO MOON

by

Peggy Thompson

Calamity Jane and the Fat Buffalo Moon was commissioned by the Canadian Broadcasting Corporation for Studio '92, and first broadcast on the CBC Stereo network on January 10, 1992, with the following cast:

Donna Goodhand (Jane)
Peter McNeill (Hickock)
John Bourgeois (Cody / Conductor)
Robert Bockstael (Duke / McCall / Gambler)
Jacqueline Samuda (Janey / Woman Two)
Kate Lynch (Woman One / Barmaid)

Produced and directed in Toronto by Baŋuta Rubess. Original music by John Millard. Casting Consultant: Linda Grearson. Recording Engineers: Glen McLaughlin and Joanne Anka. Sound effects by John Stewart. Production Assistant: Nina Callaghan. Script Editor: Ann Jansen. Executive Producer of Studio '92: Bill Lane.

Introduction

I think I was drawn to the story of Calamity Jane and the daughter she gave up for adoption because I myself was adopted. I'd never given much thought to my own birth-mother until a few years ago, then thoughts of her began to cross my mind and I began to wonder about her. Who was she? What was she like? Am I like her? Does she have curly hair and blue eyes and a poor sense of balance like me?

Around this time, my own mother, who is alarmingly psychic where I'm concerned, sat me down at the kitchen table and out of the blue told me what she had been told of my birth-mother, which wasn't much: she was in the army, became pregnant and left Toronto for Vancouver to have me. After I was born she headed back East, and our paths have never crossed again.

I found as I explored Calamity Jane's life that I had a lot of emotional connections to her story and to her daughter's story. The story of the mother and daughter who never knew each other touched me deeply, and so I've added my own few words to the myth and legend about Calamity Jane.

Martha Jane Canary was born in 1852. Maybe. Dates weren't Jane's strong suit, and we only have her word for it. She died in Deadwood, South Dakota in 1903. That's for sure. And she was buried by Wild Bill Hickock, the man she loved more than any other and whom she saw shot down in cold blood by a no-good punk. Jane claimed to be his wife and she always said that her Janey was his daughter.

Calamity Jane claimed to be a lot of things. And was many more. She dressed in men's clothes, she rode shotgun on the stage coach, she knocked about the Wild West from the time she was a kid and she lived a wild life. Jane was a scout, a thief, a nurse, a drunkard, a hero, a friend of the downtrodden, a liar and a gambler, and probably a prostitute when times got that bad. She was a performer in Buffalo Bill's Wild West Show, and she was a mother too.

Jane died only ninety years ago. But that's long enough for the lines between myth and reality to have blurred completely. The days of the Wild West weren't that long ago, and there are still people alive who met Calamity Jane, but no two accounts of her life match even remotely and they never will. And I'm sure that's how she would have wanted it.

Radio is wonderful medium to write for. In film anything is possible—for a price. In radio anything is possible. Period. And that's the joy of it.

This play is dedicated to my mother.

PEGGY THOMPSON

Characters

JANE: Calamity Jane

HICKOCK: Wild Bill Hickock

CONDUCTOR

CODY: Buffalo Bill Cody

DUKE: A Russian Duke

WOMAN ONE and WOMAN TWO

BARMAID

GAMBLER

McCALL

JANEY: Jane's daughter

Calamity Jane
AND THE FAT BUFFALO MOON

Scene One: Train Compartment

(MUSIC: "Buffalo" theme.)

(SOUND: Train and storming buffalo herds.)

JANE: *(Internal.)* August 14, 1875, Texas.

Dear Janey,

We're travelling West, Wild Bill Hickock and myself, to meet up with Buffalo Bill Cody. Oh Janey, wish you could see the buffalo herds. We've passed thousands of buffalo, so many that folks just lean out the window and shoot them from the train. You may hear Janey, that your mother was wild, but I come by it naturally. My mother and father met in an Ohio house of ill-repu—*(Cuts herself off.)*—uh, I mean a house filled with lots of wild girls. Papa swore he'd change her. Mama just swore. And she drank and had her pleasure with the men. She rode well as a man and could shoot too, better'n Papa. I believe all my blood is hers. Except the blood that made her such a beauty.

(SOUND: Train doors slamming, one after another, off.)

I am not a beauty Janey, and I hope when it comes to looks you take after your father. He's the prettiest man in the West.

(MUSIC: "Buffalo" theme out.)

HICKOCK: *(From down the corridor.)* Jane, where the hell are ya?

CONDUCTOR: *(Over HICKOCK, off.)* Fort McPherson next stop, next stop Fort McPherson.

Scene One (cont.): Train Corridor

(SOUND: Train stops, steam hisses as the door of Jane's compartment opens to corridor.)

HICKOCK: Damnation, woman!

JANE: God you're a mean-tempered devil, Bill.

HICKOCK: Where are ya? Can't see ya …

JANE: Take my arm.

HICKOCK: Lost that card game. Sure I had four kings, they were only jacks.

Scene One (cont.): Train Platform

(SOUND: Train doors swing open to a milling crowd. Porters calling.)

JANE: There's three, no four steps down … Lordy Bill, wish you'd see a doctor.

HICKOCK: No leech can save me. Blind gun-slinger is a dead man. And don't you tell Cody neither.

CODY: *(From a distance.)* Wild Bill Hickock you old rattlesnake!

HICKOCK: Cody! *(To JANE.)* Promise you won't tell. Promise.

JANE: All right, Bill. I promise.

CODY: Lord you look God Almighty fine, Bill. And you must be Calamity Jane, Queen of the Western Plains. Buffalo Bill Cody at your service.

Scene Two: Saloon

(MUSIC: Last chords of a lively bar song.)

(SOUND: Applause, saloon crowd. Clink of glasses for toast, close.)

JANE: To Hell!

HICKOCK: To Hell!

CODY: To Hell! Devil take the hindmost!

(SOUND: Drinking. Three glasses slam on table.)

(MUSIC: Saloon piano resumes in a mellow mood.)

HICKOCK: *(Belches.)* Cody, trade me places, I never sat with my back to the door before and I'm not starting in Texas.

JANE: Better do as he says—it's one of his superstitions …

CODY: Aw Bill, no one's gonna shoot you in the back …

(SOUND: A gun cocks.)

HICKOCK: That's right … 'cause I'm gonna be sittin' facing the door.

(SOUND: Chairs scrape as they change places.)

CODY: There. So, how's your shooting?

HICKOCK: Same as ever.

CODY: Tell you why I asked, I'm putting on a show about the West. Some fellers back east think we can make a fortune. I was kind of hoping you and Calamity'd be my stars. No one does shooting tricks like Wild Bill Hickock.

JANE: I'm no showgirl. And Bill, Bill doesn't want to do any more shooting for a living, do ya Bill?

HICKOCK: Sure I do.

JANE: No you don't.

HICKOCK: Damn it Jane, ain't I the fastest gun in the West?

CODY: Figure you can still make a tin can dance twenty feet across the sky?

HICKOCK: Figure I could.

(MUSIC: Saloon piano out.)

Scene Three: Fort McPherson Street

(SOUND: A busy western street, horses and carriages.)

CODY: *(From a distance.)* Ladies and gentlemen of Fort McPherson. For your afternoon's pleasure, an impromptu shooting performance by the legendary Wild Bill Hickock!

(SOUND: Curious crowd, scattered applause.)

HICKOCK: *(Aside.)* Am I pointing in the right direction, Jane?

JANE: *(Aside.)* Looks to me like you'll land one right between the mayor's eyes …

HICKOCK: Maybe my eyes ain't up to shooting today.

JANE: Maybe you're a damn fool, Bill Hickock.

HICKOCK: Aw, Jane, don't leave me … Jane!

(MUSIC: Melodramatic: "Damsel in Distress," "High Noon.")

(SOUND: JANE running across the street.)

JANE: *(Internal.)* Now, if I just got up on that roof, I might have a good angle. Of course, I've never shot a can across the sky before ...

(SOUND: JANE clambering up the side of a horse with grunts. Excited crowd in the distance.)

CODY: *(From a distance.)* On the count of three. One ... Two ...

(SOUND: JANE cocks her guns.)

JANE: *(Internal.)* Lord, hope he don't blow somebody's brains out.

CODY: *(Off.)* Three!

(MUSIC: Peaks.)

(SOUND: Guns roar, can is hit, crowd applauds.)

JANE: *(Internal, over.)* Jane, your shooting's getting better. Mama'd be proud.

(MUSIC: Relaxed "Buffalo" theme sneaks in underneath.)

CODY: *(Off.)* Wild Bill Hickock, and his amazing pistol prowess! And I'm proud to announce that Wild Bill and Calamity Jane ... *(Fades.)*

(MUSIC: "Buffalo" theme rises.)

Scene Four: The Prairie, Night

(SOUND: Coyotes howl, a camp-fire crackles close by.)

JANE: *(Internal.)* August 16th.

Dear Janey,

Cody and Bill've been hired by this hoity-toity Russian Duke Alexis, to take him out to the buffalo herds and do some shooting. We're riding with Chief Spotted Tail and his scouts. Spotted Tail told me that according to Indian legend, when the buffaloes vanish, they've run into the ground. 'Cause they live under the earth also. They must be there now, for we ain't seen hide nor hair of 'em since we started, although their bones are everywhere. The Grand Duke Alexis complains constantly and halts every three hours to drink champagne. Pretty and rich but he can't shoot worth a damn. Our moon has risen, Janey. The Sioux call it the fat buffalo moon when the moon and the buffalo are their biggest. They say for eating buffalo, the tongues are the tastiest part. Good night, Janey, till next time.

(MUSIC: "Buffalo" theme out.)

Scene Five: The Prairie, Day

(SOUND: Horses stamp, whinny and neigh. Men talk, spurs jangle as they mount up. Light wind.)

HICKOCK: Jane, ain't that sun ever gonna rise?

JANE: Sun's up Bill, been up for twenty minutes.

HICKOCK: Shite. Don't understand how the hell I shot that damn can across the sky when I can't even see the sun coming up. I ain't hunting today, tell Cody I'm sick.

JANE: You ain't never sick.

HICKOCK: *(Moving off.)* Then tell him I'm drunk 'cause I'm gonna be. *(Stomps off.)*

JANE: Bill, Bill, look out for that horse …

(SOUND: Horse rears up, neighs.)

HICKOCK: Shite!

(SOUND: Further horse noises.)

Whoa, easy there, girl … easy …

JANE: Bill, you okay?

HICKOCK: Leave me the hell alone.

(SOUND: CODY's horse pulls up.)

CODY: Jane, where's Bill? The Grand Duke's whining like a baby.

JANE: Bill can't hunt today, Cody—told me to tell you. He's uh, well, he's …

CODY: Hell. Any chance we can sober him up fast?

JANE: I wouldn't count on Bill today.

(MUSIC: "A scheme is born," sneaks in.)

CODY: Jane, the Duke ain't never seen Wild Bill. Ain't that so?

JANE: I reckon.

CODY: Well you're already in britches … if you pull your bandanna up over your face, and I say you're Wild Bill, who's to know?

JANE: 'Cept I never shot a buffalo before, Cody.

CODY: Oh it's easy as pie. Take my bandanna. Hurry up, he's coming!

(SOUND: JANE mounts her horse. DUKE's horse approaches.)

DUKE: *(Moving on.)* Cody, no more delay. We shoot the mangy buffalo. I am bored already. Why, on Taiga we have many great animals—tigers, bears, elks. Here, in West, mangy buffalo.

CODY: Count Alexis. Allow me to present Wild Bill Hickock. He'll be your guide today.

DUKE: Ah, the great Wild Bill! Yes, now, we have some manly sport, eh Hickock?

JANE: *(Gruff voice.)* Uh, we'll kill ourselves a mess of buffalo.

(SOUND: Horse moving off.)

CODY: *(Moving off.)* Enjoy your shooting, gentlemen.

JANE: *(Calling, gruff.)* Ain't you coming, Cody?

(SOUND: Horse galloping off.)

CODY: *(Calling.)* Good luck, Bill.

(MUSIC: A bridge to next scene.)

Scene Six: Great Plain

(SOUND: The thunderous roar of three hundred buffalo racing across the plains, with riders in hot pursuit. Gunshots, war whoops, the whole enchilada, moving off. Then, gunshot, close.)

DUKE: I miss again! Bill, you are not guiding me so well!

(SOUND: Gun cocks, another shot, underneath.)

JANE: *(Internal.)* Lord, he shoots like a baby. Maybe if I can get him directly in front of a buffalo he'll have a chance ... a little bullwhip on his horse might be just the ticket ... *(Aloud, gruff.)* Try this, your highness!

(SOUND: Crack of the bullwhip; his horse neighs and charges.)

DUKE: *(Moving off.)* How dare you!!! Aiee!!

(SOUND: Buffalo charge.)

JANE: *(Gruff.)* Shoot for God's sake, you yellow-bellied son of a lizard!

(SOUND: Burst of gunshots.)

(Internal.) Lord he missed again. Well, let's see if I can't just help this ninny out. *(To DUKE.)* Your highness! That big one, comin' your way! *(Internal.)* Okay, Jane, nice and easy oughta do it.

(SOUND: Herd continues racing. The DUKE fires. JANE does too.)

(Internal.) Got him in one, Jane.

DUKE: He drops. Yes!

(MUSIC: "Triumphant Hunter.")

(SOUND: Herd races off, sound fades. Horses pull up.)

JANE: Nice shot, your Highness.

DUKE: Oh he is magnificent. Here, give me your bandanna, I will cut out tongue. Bill, your bandanna to wrap up tongue!

JANE: *(Gruff.)* Uh, always keep it on …

DUKE: Oh give me …

JANE: Oh no you don't!

(SOUND: Snap of a bandanna pulled off.)

Damn!

DUKE: But you are woman, where is Wild Bill? Or is Wild Bill really woman?

JANE: Oh hell I ain't Wild Bill. I'm Calamity Jane.

(SOUND: Vulture flaps and cries above.)

DUKE: No woman takes me on hunt!

JANE: Oh yeah?

(SOUND: A gun cocks.)

You got your bull, so quit your belly-aching.

DUKE: You dare pull gun on Grand Duke! You entrance me. Come, we will drink champagne in my coach.

Scene Seven: Grand Duke's Caravan

(MUSIC: Scratchy gramophone, something Russian.)

(SOUND: The pop of a champagne cork, glasses clink, underneath.)

DUKE: Na zdrovye! *["To your health."]*

JANE: To your bull, your highness!

DUKE: So, you are married to the killer, Wild Bill …

JANE: No, no. Wild Bill ain't no killer. He was a lawman and a pony express rider. And, uh, we ain't married.

DUKE: *(Pleased.)* Oh? He does not love you?

JANE: He's got a wife already. I don't like to talk about her.

DUKE: I owe you debt of gratitude for today.

(SOUND: Jewel box opened, jewels.)

Here, a gift from my heart … you can have them if you kiss me.

JANE: Oh Lordy, those are the biggest diamonds I've ever seen. But, I can't wear jewels, Alexis. My bones are too big.

DUKE: In that case, I'll put them away.

JANE: I didn't say I didn't like them. Maybe I'll just try it here, on my arm.

DUKE: Enchanting.

JANE: You think so?

DUKE: I must kiss your arm. *(Kiss.)*

JANE: And if I put 'em here? *(Kiss.)* And here, around my throat?

DUKE: Then I must kiss your throat. *(Kiss.)* Oh, you intoxicate me.

JANE: You Russians kiss quite well …

(SOUND: A knock on the door, slightly off.)

DUKE: We'll ignore them …

(SOUND: Door opens, slightly off.)

CODY: *(Slightly off.)* Grand Duke, you'll be pleased to know … oh … *(Amused.)* 'Scuse me, "Bill" …

JANE: Oh, get outta here, Cody.

(SOUND: Door slams, slightly off.)

Now, where were we?

DUKE: The north. *(Kiss.)* The south. *(Kiss.)* And … the west. *(Kiss.)*

(MUSIC: The record finishes, sound of the needle, no one goes to get it.)

Scene Eight: Camp-fire in the Prairies

(SOUND: Fire, crickets, the soft neigh of a horse.)

(MUSIC: A harmonica is played some distance off.)

(SOUND: Footsteps moving on.)

JANE: Cody. Been looking for you.

CODY: Been waiting for you, Jane. *(Pause.)* Cat got your tongue? *(Pause.)* I ain't blabbed to Bill, if that's what you're wondering.

JANE: *(Hesitates.)* Aw hell, Bill's going blind, Cody. I swore I wouldn't tell you, but someone's gotta take him back East to doctors. Operation's his only chance. I'm no damn good in cities ... will you take him, Cody?

CODY: The whole dang town saw him shoot, Jane.

JANE: They saw *me* shoot. Bill couldn't hit the broadside of a barn. Sooner or later, word'll get out. And once it does, every tadpole in the West'll come gunning for him—to make a name for himself as "The man who killed Wild Bill Hickock."

CODY: I know a good doc in Chicago. But you know Bill. It won't be easy. Put him in a hotel and before you can say whiskey, he's broke all the furniture and shot the hell out of all the staff. God knows what'll he do in a hospital. It's gonna be expensive.

(SOUND: A necklace is pulled from a pocket.)

JANE: I'll pay, Cody. With these. And Bill mustn't know.

CODY: My God, Jane, where'd you get these diamonds? They must be worth a king's ransom.

JANE: Will you do it, Cody?

(MUSIC: Harmonica peaks.)

Scene Nine: Quiet Prairie Night

(SOUND: Dying fire, coyote howling in distance. JANE and HICKOCK kissing.)

JANE: *(Softly.)* Bill. We gotta talk, Bill. Gotta talk about the future. What are we going to do?

HICKOCK: *(Happily drunk.)* The future? We're in Cody's Western show! I'll shoot and you'll do tricks with your bullwhip!

JANE: Bill, you can't shoot. Those days are over.

HICKOCK: Sure I can. It's a damn miracle. I can't see, but I can still shoot. Remember that can? I made it dance!

JANE: I love you, Bill, and so I shot that can for ya. From the roof. I didn't want you to make a fool of yourself in front of everyone.

HICKOCK: You're a damn liar. Hold something up and I'll prove it.

JANE: Won't.

HICKOCK: The whiskey bottle. I'll crack it in two!

(SOUND: Gun shoots. Nothing is hit.)

I missed? I missed?

JANE: Cody's gonna take you to Chicago. See a doctor and maybe have an operation.

HICKOCK: You swore you wouldn't tell Cody.

JANE: Well, I lied.

HICKOCK: Damn you!

(SOUND: He grabs her.)

JANE: *(Struggling.)* Let go of me, Bill. I said let go, God damn it.

(SOUND: They scuffle, she punches him. A dog starts barking.)

HICKOCK: Ooof! Hey, get closer where I can see you.

JANE: Hate to hurt you, Bill.

(SOUND: A bottle smashes on his head. HICKOCK yells.)

You're going with Cody.

(SOUND: Stumbling steps.)

HICKOCK: *(Groans.)* I always said you were mean-spirited. Yeah, I'll go east with Cody. Gotta letter from my wife, saying she wants me back. Guess it'd be nice to have the company of a real woman for a change. *(Moving off.)* Yeah, I'll go East with Cody, Jane. And you can go to hell!

Scene Ten: Saloon

(MUSIC: Saloon music. Drunken "Buffalo" theme.)

(SOUND: A crowd, boisterous and loud.)

JANE: *(Internal.)* October 9. Deadwood Gulch.

Dear Janey,

Wild Bill Hickock is the meanest, most ornery, most chicken-hearted pole-cat ever lived. But I don't care about him. Deadwood is a damn fine town, full of gamblers, killers and brazen hussies. Only trouble is, respectable folk are takin' over and spoiling everyone's fun. A group of these so called "good ladies" have ordered me out of town. Just 'cause I drink and cuss and wear men's clothes and have my fun with their husbands.

(MUSIC: "Buffalo" theme wallows out.)

Scene Eleven: Hotel Room, Morning

(SOUND: Door opens stealthily, as JANE snores.)

WOMAN ONE: *(Over.)* She's been drinking again.

WOMAN TWO: We'll fix her wagon. Look at her men's britches.

WOMAN ONE: She smells ripe as an outhouse. Don't know what your husband sees in her, Helen.

WOMAN TWO: That will do, Gladys. Wake the Jezebel up. This is her last day in Deadwood Gulch.

WOMAN ONE: I'm scared.

WOMAN TWO: Gladys—

WOMAN ONE: *(Whimpers.)* Yes, Helen.

(SOUND: Sneaky footsteps. A glass is knocked over and rolls on the floor, the mattress creaks.)

(Whispers.) Sorry!

JANE: *(Jerks awake.)* Who the hell are you?

WOMAN TWO: Calamity Jane, we represent the God-fearing folk of Deadwood and you have five minutes to get outta town.

(SOUND: A gun cocked by an inexperienced hand.)

JANE: You pull that trigger and you're just as likely to shoot your little friend here through the gizzard as me.

WOMAN ONE: Don't shoot my gizzard, Helen!

WOMAN TWO: Everyone knows since Wild Bill left you're nothing but a drunk and a Jezebel. Gladys, grab her!

(SOUND: A tussle, screams, the gun drops to the floor.)

Grab her feet, Gladys, and we'll throw her out the window.

JANE: *(Struggling.)* Lemme go, you puss-gullied bitches!

(SOUND: Huge crash of breaking glass.)

(MUSIC: Wounded "Buffalo" theme up and then down.)

Scene Twelve: Black Hills

(SOUND: In the distance, an especially mournful coyote howls. A camp-fire, close. Cork pulled out of a whiskey bottle. JANE drinks from bottle. Smacks her lips.)

JANE: *(Internal.)* The Black Hills, May 17th, 1876.

Dear Janey,

Deadwood's sorta lost its appeal for me, so I've been prospecting for gold. Only problem is all the gold's on Indian land and there's been some blood spilt. Government offered to buy it from the Indians, but they say these hills are sacred and won't sell. People still been hunting for the gold, but if the tribes catch 'em—they'll kill 'em. Everyone says it will come to war. *(Drinks.)* The Indians never bother me. When I ride through their country, I ride standing on my head, and they think I'm plum loco and leave me alone. *(Drinks.)* Saw an unhappy sight today. A group of braves gathered around some range cattle. They were cutting the tongues out. The tribes miss the buffalo even more than the fur traders. If you ever hear from that coyote-faced Wild Bill Hickock, I want you to know that he is no friend of mine. *(She drinks, drinks, and drinks.)*

Scene Thirteen: Hotel Room

(SOUND: Muffled crowd from a saloon downstairs with someone hesitantly picking out a tune on piano.)

JANE: *(Internal.)* Deadwood Gulch.

Dear Janey.

War is upon us. Just three days ago General Custer and his men were slaughtered at Little Big Horn, not a day's ride from here. I walked the battle field after it was all over, and I pray I never see the like again. The Indian women had cut up the corpses something fierce. Legs hacked off. Arms, heads, eyes gouged out. But I can't find it in my heart to blame 'em, 'cause Custer and his men attacked an Indian village when the men were gone and raped and murdered all the women and children. I saw many friends on that field. I can't seem to write any more tonight …

(MUSIC: A bridge to next scene.)

Scene Fourteen: Saloon

(SOUND: Wild party sounds in the background. Glass down on a counter.)

JANE: 'Nother whiskey.

BARMAID: Ain't ya drunk enough, Jane?

(SOUND: A gun cocks.)

JANE: I'll tell ya when I've drunk enough.

(SOUND: Drink poured.)

BARMAID: Heard the news? Wild Bill's in town.

JANE: I don't know any varmint named Wild Bill.

BARMAID: Well, him and Cody are both here.

JANE: Are they staying upstairs?

BARMAID: Hey Jane—Jane, where ya going?

(SOUND: Footsteps running up stairs.)

(MUSIC: A bridge to next scene.)

Scene Fifteen: Hotel Room

(SOUND: Footsteps moving on.)

HICKOCK: And I do believe my four kings take the pot, boys.

JANE: Four kings will take the pot Bill, but those ain't kings, they're queens. Think you were going blind or some dang thing.

(SOUND: Money and chips swept up.)

Why don't you boys vamoose?

CODY: Bill?

HICKOCK: See ya in the morning Cody.

(SOUND: Footsteps moving off.)

GAMBLER: Good night, then.

CODY: *(Overlap.)* Bill. Night, Jane.

(SOUND: Door closes.)

JANE: So, Bill. Where's the little woman, she not with you on this journey?

HICKOCK: Oh, Jane, I've been such a damn fool.

JANE: You don't say?

HICKOCK: A settled life makes me crazier than a coyote on loco weed.

JANE: That a fact?

HICKOCK: And I missed you.

JANE: Well, I didn't miss you, not for a second.

HICKOCK: You're lying, Jane. You always were a liar.

JANE: How's your eyes, Bill.

HICKOCK: Doctors couldn't do nothing. Aw, it don't matter. My shooting days are over, I know that now.

JANE: I don't know what I ever saw in you, Bill. But whatever it was, you've still got it.

(MUSIC: A romantic bridge.)

Scene Sixteen: Hotel Room

(SOUND: Birds chirp outside the window. A light kiss, rustle of clothing and creaking mattress.)

JANE: Bill? Don't get up, Bill.

HICKOCK: Got to. *(Lying.)* Uh, Cody wants us to help him recruit folks for his Wild West Show.

JANE: No one's up yet, 'cept for the lousy tin-horns been up all night losing at poker in the bar.

HICKOCK: Well, just so happens I thought I'd try and win my money back … after I've won I'll come back up and we'll celebrate.

JANE: Give me a kiss before you go.

(SOUND: A kiss.)

HICKOCK: Jane, take my hand. A ghost just touched my heart …

JANE: Oh, poo. You always were the most superstitious man.

HICKOCK: You're right. Nothing'll happen, nothin' ever has.

(SOUND: Creaking mattress.)

JANE: Oh, I suppose I may as well come with you. Tell you what, seeing as how your eyes are so bad, maybe I can help you out some …

Scene Seventeen: Nearly Empty Saloon

(SOUND: Someone sweeping the bar-room, putting away glasses, a rooster in the distance. Cards are shuffled.)

HICKOCK: Now boys, before we start. One of you'll have to trade places with me. I never sit with my back to the wall …

CODY: Superstitious old prairie dog …

JANE: Better humour him, boys.

GAMBLER: Jack McCall says you're still the fastest draw in the West.

HICKOCK: My fighting days are over, gentlemen.

GAMBLER: That's not what Jack McCall's saying.

JANE: Jack McCall is an ignorant pup.

(SOUND: Saloon doors swing open, heavy steps.)

(MUSIC: Sudden danger.)

BARMAID: *(Under her breath.)* Uh oh, Jack McCall …

McCALL: *(Slightly off.)* Wild Bill Hickock?

(SOUND: Chairs pushed back.)

Prepare to meet your maker.

(SOUND: Gunshots. Screams. A body falls.)

JANE: Bill, Bill!

McCALL: Hah! I did it! I just shot Wild Bill! I'm the fastest gun in the West! Whiskey all around!

BARMAID: *(Off, calling outside.)* Jack McCall just shot Wild Bill!

JANE: Get your hands up, ya murdering rat. I'll see ya swing for this.

(SOUND: Crowd, some excited, some shocked, "Thanks for the whiskey," etc.)

(MUSIC: Up and down.)

Scene Eighteen: Hotel Room

(SOUND: Birds, mournful. HICKOCK breathing slow and pained.)

JANE: Bill?

HICKOCK: Jane? Jane.

JANE: Bill, don't die, please. *(Pause.)* You can't die yet Bill, I got plans for us. *(Pause.)* I love you, Bill. *(Long pause.)* Bill?

(MUSIC: Sting, then a sad country violin.)

Scene Nineteen: Graveyard

(SOUND: Cawing crow. Crowd coughs, sobs, reciting of the Lord's Prayer underneath.)

JANE: *(Internal.)* Dear Janey,

Wild Bill always aimed to kill and now he's dead. We bury him today and I don't think I can carry on. Jack McCall'll hang for his crime, but nothin'll bring Bill back to me. I've drunk two bottles of whiskey today and I'm still sober as hell. Cody's after me to join his exposition, but my heart is too black and empty for this new-fangled show business.

Scene Twenty: Saloon

(MUSIC: Jolly saloon music.)

(SOUND: Saloon crowd. Pounding on the bar, glasses rattle, close.)

JANE: More whiskey!

CODY: You've drunk enough Jane.

JANE: I'll tell you when I've had enough.

CODY: Jane, I'm telling you. If you don't come East with me, you'll drink yourself to death.

JANE: Fine.

CODY: You're leavin' this godforsaken hole now!

JANE: Lemme go, Cody! You can't make me do nothing I don't want.

Scene Twenty-one: Fairground

(MUSIC: Calliope.)

(SOUND: Western show crowd. The crunch of steps on gravel.)

CODY: Ladies and Gentlemen, welcome to Buffalo Bill's Grand Buffalo Hunt! Featuring Calamity Jane and her bullwhipping feats, the Indians of the Sacs and Fox tribes, the world famous ace-shot Annie Oakely, and the Mexican Vaquero Troupe.

And now, ladies and gentlemen, for your pleasure and edification, the opportunity, which may never come your way again, to see the one and only Calamity Jane, Queen of the Western Plains, perform amazing feats with her bullwhip. *(Internal.)* If she ain't been drinking again and don't fall off her horse.

(SOUND: A horse gallops in, rears up and whinnies.)

JANE: Howdy folks! I'm Calamity Jane!

(SOUND: The crowd cheers.)

CODY: *(Over.)* For her first trick, Calamity Jane will snap the hat offa her assistant and send it flying across the ring. On the count of three—one, two, three!

(SOUND: Crack of bullwhip. Assistant shrieks with pain. The crowd boos.)

(To himself.) Oh, Lord.

JANE: Aw, what the hell do you all know! Here, lemme get offa my horse … I'll try again … aahhh! *(She falls off her horse.)*

(SOUND: Boos and catcalls as she picks herself up.)

Oof. Shite. Okay, lemme at 'em. Where's my whip? We're gonna have a buffalo hunt!

CODY: Calamity Jane, ladies and gentlemen, the one and only! *(Aside.)* Somebody get her out of that ring now. Pull out the goddamn burning chuck-wagons. *(To crowd.)* Ladies and gentlemen *(Fading.)* and now a historic tableaux of the battle of …

Scene Twenty-two: Backstage, Wild West Show

(MUSIC: Calliope in the distance.)

(SOUND: The fairground in the distance.)

JANE: Oh Cody. Let me go home to Deadwood.

CODY: Can't go home, our next show's in Richmond and you've still got top billing.

JANE: Richmond? Oh, I can't go to Richmond.

CODY: Why the hell not?

JANE: My daughter Janey's in Richmond. She can't see me like this … doing bad shooting and terrible riding …

CODY: Well then, get off the drink and pull yourself together.

(MUSIC: Vibrant "Buffalo" theme swells.)

Scene Twenty-three: Train Compartment

(SOUND: Train.)

JANE: *(Internal, cheerful and strong.)* Travelling West …

Dear Janey,

I saw you watching me doing tricks with my old bullwhip. Your eyes like saucers. I wasn't drunk so carried off my part as well as I ever could. Captain Jim brought you backstage after in your pretty pink dress, and I asked who your mother was, and you said, "Oh, I am an orphan," and you put your arms around my neck and kissed me on the lips the way I used to kiss my Ma. Maybe I haven't been such a bad sort after all.

(SOUND: Train goes through a level crossing.)

(MUSIC: "Buffalo" theme out.)

Scene Twenty-three (cont.): Train

CODY: I've been hearing some rumours you're leaving, Jane.

JANE: Oh Cody, I ain't done nothing right in your show.

CODY: It's true. You're my worst performer, Jane. But there's only a few of us left from the old days. Remember that buffalo hunt, remember when the prairie'd turn black with buffalo?

JANE: So many buffalo, folks'd just cut their tongues out and leave the rest.

CODY: Bones are all that's left now. You know there's great trade in buffalo bones. Businessmen scoop 'em up, send 'em East on the train, and they're baked and pulverized, and added to sugar. Sugar's sent west and Western folk drink it in their coffee.

JANE: We're getting old, Cody.

CODY: We're dying off just like buffalo. We thought it'd last forever. But it's gone, like a dream you know was grand but can't remember.

(MUSIC: Soft, gently up and then down.)

Scene Twenty-four: Shack

(SOUND: Wind blowing outside and rattling windows, a creaking rocking chair.)

JANE: *(Internal.)* Black Hills, December 1903.

Dear Janey,

My time has come and this will be my last letter to you, my dear daughter. Seems I'm going blind. I no longer see what's in front of my face, but things from long ago. Wild Bill's been with me these last few days. He just sits on a chair and don't move. Silent as the grave. It's so cold, Janey, so damn cold where I'm going and I'm scared. Really scared for the first time in my life. Please know my last thoughts are with you.

(SOUND: A train goes by.)

Jane, that night of your birth, I held you in my arms. I loved you so, I cried like a baby myself. Bill didn't believe you were his child, though you were. I left you with Captain Jim and his family to raise, so I could keep the man I loved. I've done some wicked acts in my life, but leaving you behind was the only thing I ever regret. Forgive me.

(MUSIC: A flourish.)

(SOUND: Coyotes howl, wind blows very fiercely, shutters rattle.)

Scene Twenty-five: Cheery Kitchen

(SOUND: Birds chirping, teapot whistling and taken off.)

(MUSIC: Finale sneaks in underneath.)

JANEY: *(Internal.)* Black Hills, 1910.

Dear Momma,

I went to where you were buried today, right beside Wild Bill. It's a popular spot. Many people come to visit you both. Old timers here still tell stories about you. Calamity Jane, the Beautiful White Devil of the Hills. Calamity Jane, the Heroine of the Plains. Rescuer of the Deadwood Stage Coach. Champion Cusser. Bullwhipper. And Brazen Hussy. I'll always remember the day I saw you in Cody's show. I thought you were the most brave and beautiful woman I'd ever seen. Folks round here say I look just like you.

Your loving daughter, Janey.

(MUSIC: Finale rises and ends.)

Nellie Bly

Ten Days in a Madhouse

by

Beverley Cooper

Nellie Bly: Ten Days in a Madhouse was commissioned by the Canadian Broadcasting Corporation for Studio '93, and first broadcast on the CBC Stereo network on March 5, 1993, with the following cast:

Lindsey Leese (Nellie)
David Fox (Pulitzer)
John Jarvis (Cockerill / Driver / Dr Kinier)
Sandi Ross (Nurse Snipe)
Janet Burke (Tillie)
Miriam Newhouse (Mrs. Neville)
Beverley Cooper (Birgit / Mrs. Stanard)
Victoria Mitchell (Miss Cherube / Mother / Attendant)

Produced and directed in Toronto by Baŋuta Rubess. Original music by Lesley Barber. Casting Consultant: Linda Grearson. Recording Engineer: Joanne Anka. Sound effects by Joe Hill. Production Assistant: Kate Nickerson. Script Editor: Ann Jansen. Executive Producer of Studio '93: Bill Lane.

Introduction

My family has a cherished cottage in beautiful British Columbia, deep in the heart of the Kootenays. The summers that I spent there as a child are remembered as one glorious blur. However I do have one particularly fond memory that has to do with CBC radio. The CBC AM channel was our one link with the outside world—surprise!—no TV, no telephone. One summer, CBC was replaying an old radio soap opera. Monday to Friday I would listen to the crackling sounds on the big old radio while I did the breakfast dishes, waiting for the water to heat up on the wood stove. What I remember most is the wonderful style the radio drama presented; how I could use my imagination to see those vivid characters; how the music swelled with emotion; how the sound effects swept the stories forward. I have always loved that old-time radio style.

Now as a writer, I am still fascinated with that style, but what really interests me is how I can use that style, warp that style for my own purpose: to tell the stories I want to tell, to expose the outrages of life while clothing them as entertainment. The story I want to tell with *Nellie Bly: Ten Days in a Madhouse* is the tale of an independent woman who went against the system and won.

Nellie was a plucky gal. She was born in 1862 to a well-to-do family, but when her father died she and her mother were left penniless. The choices offered to her were slim—she could get married, quick, and be dependant on her husband, or she could get so called "women's work," as a governess or as slave labour in a factory. Nellie would have none of it. She wanted to write for a newspaper so she did—this in an age when female reporters were almost unknown! She was extremely daring: travelling to Mexico to reveal the plight of the poor, going undercover to expose corrupt government officials and supporting new reforms for women. Nellie Bly's claim to fame was travelling alone around the world in a record-breaking seventy-two days. Her dispatches caught the world's attention. All this before she was thirty.

I chose to narrow in on this particular journalistic coup, Nellie reporting the conditions of New York City's horrendous insane asylum, because it was exciting, full of adventure and was typical of Nellie's fight for the underdogs of society. Also, the story lends itself to that old-time radio style: New York City in 1887, the purple prose of her writing, and the gothic feeling of the insane asylum. At the same time, the story chronicles Nellie Bly's outrage at society's wrongs as she struggled to do something about them.

BEVERLEY COOPER

Characters

NELLIE: Nellie Bly

MOTHER: Nellie's mother

PULITZER: Joseph Pulitzer, owner of the New York World

COCKERILL: Pulitzer's editor

MRS STANARD and MISS CHERUBE: Boarding-house landladies

DRIVER

NURSE SNIPE: Nurse at Blackwell's Island Lunatic Asylum

DR KINIER: Doctor at Blackwell's Island

TILLIE, BIRGIT and MRS NEVILLE: Blackwell's Island inmates

ATTENDANT

Nellie Bly

Ten Days in a Madhouse

Scene One: Montage

(MUSIC: Splashy, underneath.)

(SOUND: Typing.)

NELLIE: *(Internal.)* "Spunky Young Reporter Rises to the Top" ... "It's a Woman! New York's Best Reporter a Twenty-year-old Girl!" ... "Riveting, Radical Reporter is Tip Top Twenty Game Golden Gal!" ... Game golden gal? Hmmm.

MOTHER: *(Off.)* Nellie Bly, stop that racket and get to these dishes.

(SOUND: Typing stops.)

NELLIE: *(Internal.)* Drat. "Game Golden Gal Succumbs Sorrily to Mother's Suds."

(MUSIC: "Newspaper" theme, jazzy and fast, rises.)

Scene Two: Newspaper Office

(SOUND: A busy newspaper office.)

PULITZER: Cockerill, get in here!

(SOUND: Steps approach, a door is slammed, muffling the outer office sounds.)

COCKERILL: Yes, Mr. Pulitzer, sir?

PULITZER: *(Growling.)* Sit down. What the hell is this?

(SOUND: Newspaper snaps open.)

COCKERILL: Why that's the editorial I wrote last week. I'm sure you approved it, I—

PULITZER: Read it!

COCKERILL: Umm … "What Girls Are Good For" … uh … "There has recently been an unfortunate fad of women aiming to find work outside of the home …"

PULITZER: Stop. Read this.

COCKERILL: Oh, uh … "To the editor, shame on you! Girls are only fit for cooking and needlepoint? What kind of malarkey is that? What if I say men are only good for making money and playing sports? Working out of the home is not some silly hobby designed to embarrass men. Think about the women who have no choice, who have lost a husband, have children to support or simply find themselves not wanting to be totally dependent on a man? What do you suggest to these hard-done-by creatures … needlepoint?!"

(SOUND: A swivel chair turns.)

PULITZER: Enough. Find me the guy who wrote that.

COCKERILL: But it's anonymous, sir—

PULITZER: I know it's anonymous. Put your thinking cap on! Put an ad in the paper, walk the streets of New York, I don't care what, 'cause, quite frankly, Cockerill, this poor slob writes better than you do and if I have to find him myself he might just get the job of Editor in Chief at the New York *World.*

COCKERILL: *(Moving off.)* Oh … yes! Don't you worry, boss. Yes! Right away. I'll find this slob all right.

(SOUND: Steps moving away, a door closing.)

PULITZER: *(Under his breath.)* Perhaps *you* should take up needlepoint, Cockerill.

(SOUND: Door opening.)

COCKERILL: Uh … Mr. Pulitzer … should I print this letter?

PULITZER: You kidding?! No! Get outta here.

(MUSIC: "Newspaper" theme, fast and jazzy, time passing.)

Scene Three: Newspaper Office

(SOUND: Muffled office sounds, a knock on the door.)

PULITZER: *(Calling.)* State your business.

(SOUND: Door opening, office sounds louder.)

COCKERILL: There's a young woman to see you, boss. You won't believe it. She couldn't be more than twenty—slip of a thing, says she's some kind of a newspaper reporter looking for a job. We tried to get rid of her but—

PULITZER: A woman? Can't you see I'm busy?

COCKERILL: But boss, she's been sitting downstairs three hours—says she won't budge till you see her.

PULITZER: A lady reporter, eh?

COCKERILL: She's got spunk—might be a story herself.

PULITZER: Enough already, bring her in.

COCKERILL: *(Slightly off.)* Miss Bly ... this is Mr. Pulitzer.

(SOUND: Rustling skirts enter. The door shuts.)

NELLIE: Finally! I told them you asked to see me, but those dimwits didn't believe me. What did they think I was going to do to you—needlepoint you to death? I don't care if you are the owner I—

PULITZER: Needlepoint? Hold on. You say I asked to see you?

NELLIE: Your ad! I wrote the letter to the editor. You asked to see the author. I am she!

COCKERILL: Holy cow!

PULITZER: Have a chair ... Miss?

NELLIE: Nellie Bly.

(SOUND: A match striking, a chair pulled up, rustling skirts settle.)

PULITZER: *(Puffing on a cigar.)* Miss Bly, what do you think about writing for the *World*? It'd be novel, having a gal ... What'd ya think, Cockerill? ... Maybe she could cover the theatre, check out the bake sales ...

NELLIE: Mr. Pulitzer. I've been a reporter at *The Pittsburgh Dispatch* for two years.

PULITZER: Never heard of ya.

NELLIE: Do you read the *Dispatch*?

PULITZER: No.

NELLIE: Well then.

COCKERILL: I heard of ya! The lady at the *Dispatch,* yeah!

PULITZER: Continue.

NELLIE: Mr. Pulitzer, I'd like to work for you but I'm not a gossip columnist, I'm a journalist!

PULITZER: I don't know what kind of stories we could give a lady like yourself. New York is a rough town.

NELLIE: I've got ideas springing out of my head! I could expose the sweatshops or write about divorce or how about this? "Blackwell's Island Insane Asylum—The True Story!"

(MUSIC: Light intro to "Asylum" theme, creeps underneath.)

PULITZER: You're full of pig manure—no one gets in there.

NELLIE: *(Full of drama.)* "Young journalist pretends to be crazy to expose the hellish, horrific conditions of Blackwell's Island—home for the tragically insane." It would make a gripping story—there's hundreds of women there, all stark raving mad!

PULITZER: *(Growling.)* Get to the point, young lady.

NELLIE: I'll pretend to be loony, I'll get myself committed.

PULITZER: You're out of your mind already! You're just a kid.

NELLIE: *(On a roll.)* You can get me out after a week, or ten days. Mr. Pulitzer, my last assignment was reporting from Mexico, surely I can survive one of our city's institutions for a few days.

COCKERILL: Wow, it would make a great story, boss.

(SOUND: Chair pushed back, pacing steps.)

PULITZER: *(Pacing.)* All right. But if you get yourself in a fix, don't go crying to your Mama that I talked you into this.

NELLIE: Mr. Pulitzer, I am going to ignore that insulting remark and get you the best story this paper ever had. Just make sure you get me out of there.

(MUSIC: Jazzy and upbeat, slides underneath.)

(Internal.) September 21, 1887. "Bullish Bly Bags Work at Wonderful *World*." *(A squeal of delight.)*

(MUSIC: Still upbeat, busy.)

Scene Four: Nellie's Apartment

(SOUND: A key in the door, the door opens, a rustling skirt. A Siamese cat meows and a paper bag is unfolded.)

NELLIE: Hello, Calamity. Look what I've got. Mmmm. Liver! Hello?! Ma? *(No answer.)* Good, I can make a quick get-away.

(SOUND: Paper put into a typewriter and typing.)

"Dearest Ma,

I'm off on an assignment for the New York *World*! Yes it's true. Please feed Calamity. And if old Finnegan wants his rent money, tell him I'll pay him with interest next week. Don't worry. Exclamation mark. I'm invincible and after this I'll be famous too! Your best daughter, Nells."

(SOUND: She pulls the paper out of the typewriter.)

All right, all right, all right. The assignment! "Loony Lady Lies Way Into Lonely Loonybin."

(SOUND: Calamity meows and NELLIE feeds her.)

(Changing her voice.) Do you think I'm craaazy, Calamity? Perhaps they should lock me up in the attic and push my food under the door … ehhhh Calamiteeee?

(SOUND: Terrified, Calamity squawks and runs away. NELLIE laughs: a fiendish, insane laugh.)

(MUSIC: Gothic and disturbing, building, then suddenly out.)

Scene Five: A Cheap Boarding-house

(SOUND: The clink of teacups, a clock ticking and the creak of a rocking chair.)

NELLIE: *(Off.)* Fifteen, sixteen, seventeen … *(Continuing underneath.)*

MRS STANARD: *(She blows her nose.)* Who's the one in the corner?

MISS CHERUBE: Calls herself Nellie Brown. Came here this morning, said she was looking for a cheap boarding-house … Well, I says to her, if, by the word cheap, you mean inexpensive, then the Temporary Home for Females is what you're looking for … She just stared at me, put seventy-three cents in my palm and has been sitting there, counting, ever since; like a China doll in a store window—with glass eyes and a hollow head.

MRS STANARD: I better see what she's about.

(SOUND: The creak of couch springs, steps toward NELLIE.)

NELLIE: *(Moving on.)* … twenty-one, twenty-two, twenty-three …

MRS STANARD: What's wrong dear? Have you some sorrow or trouble?

NELLIE: Yes, everything is so sad.

MRS STANARD: We all have our troubles, but we get over them in time. What kind of work are you trying to get?

NELLIE: I never worked. I don't know how.

MRS STANARD: But you must learn. All these women work.

(MUSIC: Gothic horror.)

NELLIE: *(In a strange voice.)* Do they? They look horrible to me. Did you know half the world is full of axe murderers? They're waiting in the wings, dancing in the shadows, eyeing our necks. *(Loud sob.)*

MRS STANARD: I see. Poor loon! She'll murder us all before evening.

NELLIE: *(Internal.)* "Nellie Bly Nominated for Prestigious Acting Award." *(Aloud.)* Twenty-four, twenty-five! *(Internal.)* Twenty-five cockroaches over the obstacle course to the kitchen. I better speed up the process before I have to stay for lunch.

(SOUND: NELLIE claps her hands.)

(Screaming.) Where is my snake?! The crazy women took him. They're all crazy ... his fangs are sharp and sure but his skin is shiny and sleek!

MISS CHERUBE: Oh my word.

MRS STANARD: I better call the police.

(SOUND: Clanging of bells in the distance, horses' hooves; melodramatic "Here come the police" sounds.)

NELLIE: *(Internal.)* "Destitute Woman With No Past Found Insane—Nutty as a Fruitcake, Batty as a Bird." "Unknown Woman Sent To Blackwell's Island."

Scene Six: Countryside

(MUSIC: A melancholy intro.)

(SOUND: Desolate countryside. Horses pulling a wagon, a crow caws loudly.)

NELLIE: *(Internal.)* "As the cart rumbles towards the looming, impenetrable walls of the insane asylum, the reporter glances at her travelling companions; their lives now narrowed to the grim reality of spending the rest of their lives in this horrendous place. *(Full of drama.)* Perhaps it would be easier to walk a straight line to the gallows than to meander to this tomb of living horrors ..." *(Sniffing, aloud.)* Ughhh! What's that stench?

DRIVER: That's the kitchen, ladies, wonder what's for dinner? Boiled brains maybe. *(He laughs.)*

NELLIE: *(Internal.)* "Wizened Wino Whips Wicked Wit."

(SOUND: The horse and wagon come to a stop.)

DRIVER: That's it girls. Blackwell's Island Lunatic Asylum. Last stop for paradise. *(Mean snigger.)*

(SOUND: The women climb off the cart.)

NELLIE: This place is huge. Are there that many crazies in the whole world?

TILLIE: Tell me, Miss, do you know if there's any way I could get a message out to my sister, she's going to be sick with worry.

NELLIE: I'm afraid I don't know. May I ask your name?

TILLIE: Tillie ... Tillie Maynard. You know, I keep worrying about all the little things—like who will pay my bills or feed my cat.

NELLIE: Oh, I love cats. What kind do you have?

TILLIE: A grand Persian mix named Tybalt, after that character by Mr. Shakespeare.

NELLIE: You don't seem crazy to me.

DRIVER: Come on, in you go.

(SOUND: DRIVER spanks NELLIE, who protests as he laughs.)

TILLIE: Goodness, that man ... spanked you. I just—

(SOUND: The women are pushed inside, then the door is shut and locked with a resounding echo.)

NELLIE: *(Gasps.)* My dear God, this is it.

(MUSIC: "Insanity" theme, sneaks in.)

Scene Seven: Waiting-room

(SOUND: Footsteps shuffling into a small room, women whisper and mutter amongst themselves.)

NURSE SNIPE: In you get, there's room for all. Wait till you're called. You be nice to the doctor, and he'll be nice to you. *(She laughs.)* Very nice.

NELLIE: *(Internal.)* "The intrepid reporter is locked in, day and night behind the unmerciful bolts and bars of a loonybin. One barmy woman stares with such intensity at the ceiling that the back of her neck could snap in two. However, not all seem insane ... Tillie Maynard looks as sane as the day is long—"

TILLIE: *(From the office next door.)* I have been sick for some time ... but not in my head ... in my lungs, I'm high-strung, that's all ... if you please, give me any test for insanity.

DR KINIER: *(From the office next door.)* Demented, with delusions of persecution. Send in the next one.

(SOUND: TILLIE weeps loudly. Door opens. A small scuffle.)

NELLIE: *(Internal.)* "Barren of a judge or jury, Tillie Maynard is convicted to life in this prison. Sanity is but in the eyes of the beholder. Our intrepid reporter decides to act perfectly normal, perfectly sane. What will be the diagnosis of these so-called experts? 'Illusions of grandeur' perhaps?"

NURSE SNIPE: Nellie Brown.

(MUSIC: A high note of suspense.)

Scene Eight: Office

(SOUND: Vials clink, drawers open. NURSE SNIPE hums as she cleans and arranges instruments.)

DR KINIER: How old are you?

NELLIE: Twenty last May.

(SOUND: Writing.)

DR KINIER: Measure her.

NURSE SNIPE: You know I can't use this measuring thingamabob.

DR KINIER: Yes, you can. Go ahead, what height? *(They both laugh.)* All right, let me help you.

(SOUND: Clink of measuring device, clothing rustles. NURSE SNIPE giggles.)

Five feet, five inches.

NURSE SNIPE: *(More giggling.)* You're getting too fresh.

DR KINIER: *(To NURSE SNIPE.)* What time are you going to supper?

NELLIE: I don't want to interrupt anything important but, if you care, I am not insane, my brain is in working order, shipshape.

DR KINIER: Send in the next one.

NELLIE: I have rights! You can't shut me up here.

(SOUND: NELLIE is pushed out of the office and into a room. The door shuts behind her. More laughter is heard.)

Scene Nine: Waiting-room

NELLIE: *(Calling.)* That's not an examination, that's an insult! When I get out of here, I'll—

(SOUND: The door reopens slightly off.)

NURSE SNIPE: *(Slightly off.)* Brown, out into the hall! Don't you want to eat or … are you going to be trouble?

Scene Ten: Hallway

(MUSIC: "Shuffling Feet" theme, underneath.)

(SOUND: Feet shuffling, voices whispering, distant moaning.)

NELLIE: *(Internal.)* "Intrepid girl reporter loses round one. She stands in the hall, wind and cold whistling through, shivering with the crazy captives chattering nonsenses to invisible persons." *(Aloud.)* How long do we have to wait? Excuse me, what's your name?

BIRGIT: Birgit. Hey, who are you? Goddamned slut spy! Come to shame us all. Pig girl. Oink oink.

NELLIE: *(Internal.)* "Girl Reporter Strangled by Hostile Hog Hater."

MRS NEVILLE: *(Elderly.)* Don't mind them, dearie, they're all mad. Oh, here we go.

(SOUND: Doors opening, and the women rushing for the dining room.)

NURSE SNIPE: Get in line, two by two! Dinner time! Stop pushing like animals.

(MUSIC: "Asylum" theme, a segue to next scene.)

Scene Eleven: Dining-room

(SOUND: Pandemonium. Women's voices in a large room, munching and banging plates—they have no utensils. Some women sound quite mad. Gobbling and grabbing.)

NELLIE: Five prunes and some bread? What's this pinkish-looking stuff?

BIRGIT: *(With her mouth full.)* Tea.

NELLIE: *(Sniffing the butter.)* The butter's rancid.

BIRGIT: *(Munching.)* Gimme that.

MRS NEVILLE: *(Low.)* You must force the food down, else you'll be sick, and who knows what, with these surroundings you may go crazy.

NELLIE: I'd say these gals have already lost the battle.

MRS NEVILLE: Some are unhappy, some lonely, desperate, confused … all are hungry, cold and sick. Hidden from the world and forgotten.

TILLIE: My sister always says, "To have a good brain the stomach must be cared for."

NELLIE: How did you come to get here, Tillie?

TILLIE: I had pneumonia and was put in the mental ward by mistake. The more I complained the crazier they thought I was. They finally sent me here.

NELLIE: My god! We have to get you out.

MRS NEVILLE: No good, dearie.

(SOUND: A chair knocked over; a plate falls to the floor.)

TILLIE: *(Screams and gags.)* A … spider. I ate a spider … bread … *(Moving off.)* Mmmm …

(SOUND: Clatter of footsteps moving off.)

NURSE SNIPE: Tillie Maynard, come back!

(SOUND: A struggle as TILLIE is yanked back and hit.)

ATTENDANT: *(Grunting.)* Behave, little girl!

NELLIE: No!

MRS NEVILLE: Young lady, if you try and stop them they'll hit her harder. Don't get involved.

NURSE SNIPE: All of you, line up! Bath time!

(SOUND: Shuffling feet mingling.)

(MUSIC: "Shuffling Feet" theme, marching. The music and shuffles get louder, then stop suddenly.)

Scene Twelve: Bathroom

(SOUND: Several leaky faucets.)

NELLIE: *(Internal.)* "Adventures in a hellish washroom. The true, but tragic tale of a reporter who gets into a bathtub never to be seen again under the thick dirty water. Patients with oozing eruptions all over their bodies ... drying themselves with communal towels. A disgusting ... nasty sight—"

NURSE SNIPE: Miss Brown. Come forward and undress.

NELLIE: I don't need a bath, had one just the other day, I like a little dirt, keeps me warm'n cosy.

NURSE SNIPE: I think she wants a little help, Birgit?

BIRGIT: Oink, oink.

NELLIE: No. I can do it myself.

(SOUND: Clothes being shed.)

NURSE SNIPE: Everything off, *espec-c-c-ially* the panties.

NELLIE: No.

(SOUND: Struggle as NURSE SNIPE forces the final garment off NELLIE. NELLIE shrieks and jumps into the tub. She shrieks even more at the cold water.)

BIRGIT: I'm your washer woman, slut girl. *(Wicked chuckle.)* You look far too clean to me.

NELLIE: With that filthy rag? Ow! *(Shivering.)* Do you have to scrub so hard? Owwwww!

(SOUND: BIRGIT laughs fiendishly.)

NURSE SNIPE: Shut up or she'll give it to you worse.

(SOUND: Cold water splashes.)

NELLIE: *(Gulps for air.)* I can't breathe!

(SOUND: Another bucket is thrown. NELLIE sputters and shivers.)

I'm drowning!

NURSE SNIPE: *(Grunting.)* No lolly-gagging.

(SOUND: NELLIE is yanked from the tub.)

NELLIE: *(Shivering, internal.)* "Intrepid girl reporter found to be a fool." Must be insane to come here for a bloody story! Look at these pathetic creatures, this is their life. Absurd life, life's absurd!

(SOUND: NELLIE laughs to herself.)

(MUSIC: "Insanity" theme, sneaks underneath.)

NURSE SNIPE: Put this on.

(SOUND: Rustle of clothing.)

NELLIE: *(Reading.)* "Lunatic Asylum, Blackwell's Island, Hall Six." I guess that's for if I ever lose my way, wander away, run for the hills … Owwww! *(Screams in pain.)*

(MUSIC: "Insanity" theme out.)

BIRGIT: Hold still, slut, hair is tangled, see?

NURSE SNIPE: Come forward, Tillie Maynard.

TILLIE: Please, I've been dreadfully ill. I don't think getting my head wet will do me much good, I—

(SOUND: A bucket of water is thrown on TILLIE.)

NELLIE: Didn't you hear her?!

(SOUND: NELLIE struggles with NURSE SNIPE.)

NURSE SNIPE: Get your clammy hands off me!

(SOUND: NURSE SNIPE pushes NELLIE off.)

(MUSIC: "Melancholy" theme, up and growing darker.)

Scene Thirteen: Hall In Asylum

(SOUND: Footsteps walking along the hall.)

NURSE SNIPE: You have to be in a room alone tonight, for I suppose you're noisy and bad.

(SOUND: A door is unlocked.)

Scene Fourteen: Cell

NELLIE: Please! Could I at least have a towel to dry my hair?

NURSE SNIPE: You are in a public institution now and you should be thankful for what you get.

(SOUND: A door closes and locks. Footsteps walking off down the hall.)

(Moving off.) Nighty night, now.

(MUSIC: "Melancholy" theme out.)

(SOUND: The wind whistling outside.)

Scene Fifteen: Cell

NELLIE: *(Internal.)* "The reporter is soaking wet in an icy room with a … short, oily wool blanket …" I'll catch my death …

(SOUND: Distant voices overlap, shrieks, crying and snores: "It's so cold!" "Nurse!" "Murder!" "Fire!" "Police!" "Please God let me die!" Sounds continue underneath.)

(Internal.) Fire ... would the reporter be able to escape? The last thing these jailers would think of is releasing their crazy patients. We'd all roast to death ... or die of panic, trampling each other like rats in a cage.

(SOUND: A small animal scurries.)

Like rats. Rats! A rat! *(She screams.)*

(SOUND: Heavy footsteps return. Keys jangle, the cell door opens.)

There's a rat!

NURSE SNIPE: Drink this.

NELLIE: *(Sniffing.)* What is it?

NURSE SNIPE: It'll help you sleep.

NELLIE: No thank you.

(SOUND: NURSE SNIPE tries to force NELLIE to drink; NELLIE struggles.)

No!

NURSE SNIPE: If you don't drink it I shall inject it into your arm with a needle.

(SOUND: NELLIE slurps.)

That's a good girl.

(SOUND: The door is closed and locked. Footsteps move away; NELLIE spits out the liquid.)

NELLIE: *(Aloud.)* Must keep my wits. Must remember every detail ... "One Week in a Madhouse, by Nellie Bly. I often felt superior to those who are called insane until I was one of them." You idiot. What did you expect? I'd sit in the corner and simply observe, sipping tea ... talking to myself, I'll fit right in. My dear lord, a week in purgatory. One week. It's just one week ...

(MUSIC: "Asylum" theme dances crazily.)

Scene Sixteen: Cell

(SOUND: Distorted, frightening steps marching up the hall. Banging on the doors with a stick. The cell door is unlocked.)

NURSE SNIPE: Up, up!

(SOUND: Rustle of straw, a rooster crows. NELLIE wakes groggily)

(MUSIC: "Shuffling Feet" theme.)

(SOUND: Shuffling feet slowly increase underneath.)

NELLIE: *(Internal.)* Day two. Day three, Tillie Maynard's nowhere to be found ... day four. Breakfast at five bloody thirty in the morning ... what's the point ... A saucer of oatmeal and bread that's no more than dried dough ... lining up ... freezing cold ... shuffling along, shuffle, shuffle, shuffle.

(SOUND: Shuffling feet abruptly out.)

(MUSIC: Abruptly out with the shuffling feet.)

Scene Seventeen: Courtyard

(SOUND: The wind whistles, a crow caws.)

NURSE SNIPE: Come on, move around a bit ... you never seen daylight before?

(SOUND: A few women's feet crunching on cold ground, wandering aimlessly. In the distance, muffled moans, trudging feet coming closer.)

NELLIE: Who are they?

(MUSIC: A softer, haunting version of "Insanity" theme; mingled with:)

(SOUND: A jumble of women's voices: gibberish, cursing, singing, praying, preaching.)

MRS NEVILLE: They're the most violent—from the Lodge ... you don't want to be locked up over there. No, you don't. From what I hear, it's a nasty bit of business.

NELLIE: Do they have to lock them together like cattle?

BIRGIT: *(Totally insane.)* Let me run! My mother the god, the queen will punish you! You heathen sinners! Let me ruuuuuunn! *(Lunging at NELLIE.)* Ahahhh!

(SOUND: Steps jumping back; NELLIE gasps.)

(Sickly sweet.) Sucky baby. Scare you? *(Laughs.)*

(SOUND: Women trudge past.)

NELLIE: Tillie! Where have you been? I looked all over for you, I thought you'd been released ... Tillie?

TILLIE: *(In a daze.)* I was sent to the Lodge … because … I talked to a … man? They put me on the rope gang. The nurses beat me, choked me, kicked me, pulled my hair, held me under water … injected me with morphine … my thoughts were so … the doctors always said it was … my diseased brain … what about my kitty … do you think Tybalt's all right?

NELLIE: Oh … Tillie … *(Internal.)* "Tragic Tale of Woe; Blackwell's Island a Cesspool of Inhumanity to Women."

(SOUND: The trudging feet grow more distant, blending with music.)

(MUSIC: "Insanity" theme, up and down.)

Scene Eighteen: Sitting-room

(SOUND: Clock ticking. NELLIE coughs.)

NURSE SNIPE: Sit up and sit still!

NELLIE: Day bloody eight. Where the hell is Pulitzer? He couldn't care less about intrepid girl reporter.

NURSE SNIPE: *(Threatening.)* You talking to yourself again, Brown? I thought we had a little chat about that.

NELLIE: I was wondering, Miss Snipe. If anyone had come asking for me? To take me home, maybe?

NURSE SNIPE: Oh, now that you mention it, yes there was. A tall gentleman, handsome, wanted to speak to you.

NELLIE: There was?

NURSE SNIPE: I told him you weren't receiving any callers today.

NELLIE: You didn't! No!

NURSE SNIPE: *(Striking NELLIE.)* Sit! Can't you take a little joke?

NELLIE: Yes, Nurse Snipe, I forgot myself again, sorry, Miss. I was foolish to ask. I'm sitting down now, see, right here.

(SOUND: Couch creaks. Hard shoes walk away and stumble against a chair. TILLIE moans.)

(Whispers.) Tillie, is that you? You look awful.

TILLIE: *(Shaking with cold.)* Nellie!

NELLIE: *(Whispers.)* Shhhh.

TILLIE: *(Coughing.)* Did you talk to the doctors about me?

NELLIE: I tried, Tillie, they don't seem to listen.

TILLIE: Liar.

NELLIE: Pardon?

TILLIE: You tell them to ignore me, don't you? To lock me up and freeze me out. *(Coughing.)* You want all the attention for yourself.

NELLIE: No—

TILLIE: *(Screaming.)* You're a horrid, wicked liar! *(Coughing, unable to breathe.)*

(SOUND: TILLIE collapses. The women gasp and jump to help her.)

ATTENDANT: She's fainted.

NURSE SNIPE: Don't help her, teach her a lesson. Get up.

TILLIE: *(Gasping for air.)* For God's sake, don't let them beat me!

NURSE SNIPE: Shut up you idiot! Get up!

(SOUND: TILLIE shrieks as she is pulled up by her hair and then choked.)

NELLIE: *(Grabbing NURSE SNIPE.)* Stop! You're going to kill her!

NURSE SNIPE: Get your hands off of me.

(SOUND: They struggle, NELLIE falls down, chairs fall over.)

MRS NEVILLE: *(Low.)* They'll send you to the Lodge! You must keep still.

(SOUND: TILLIE screams as she is dragged off. The women murmur, underneath.)

NELLIE: I'm getting out of here Miss Neville ... I'm a reporter and I'm going to tell the world what is going on in here. These bloody villains aren't going to get away with this!

MRS NEVILLE: Oh, dear Nellie, you're losing your wits. Grab hold of them.

NURSE SNIPE: Sit down! All of you.

NELLIE: *(Crying to herself.)* How much more?

Scene Nineteen: Montage

(MUSIC: "Shuffling Feet" and "Insanity" themes mix together, time passing, and continue underneath.)

(SOUND: The rope gang.)

NELLIE: *(Walking.)* Day eight, or is it nine or twelve? Pulitzer's forgotten me for a better story. What did we agree upon ... remember Nellie, you idiot ... fool! Oh Ma ... you should worry. They're going around and around and around and around!

(SOUND: The shuffling feet, the haunting moans, distant cries, mad voices, underneath.)

BIRGIT: Lucifer, Lucifer—I have killed the devil ...

TILLIE: *(Her voice comes through all this, underneath and off.)* Tybalt! Alas poor Tybalt!

NELLIE: Tillie! No! ... like cattle. Let me out, let me out.

(SOUND: Doors shut and locked.)

TILLIE: Nellie! Nellie!

(MUSIC: Builds underneath.)

NELLIE: Insane, indignity ... injustice, inhumane ... *(Loudly.)* Has Mr. Pulitzer called for me?

(SOUND: The nurses whispering and laughing, underneath.)

Hungry, dirty, cold, stiff bones. Stop that talking. Quiet ... some quiet. Get these sounds out. Bursting! *(Screams.)* Get them out!

NURSE SNIPE: *(Interrupts.)* Nellie Brown? There's someone here to see you. Seems like you're going home.

(SOUND: Shuffling footsteps turn into NELLIE's footsteps, as she gradually speeds up to a run, down the hall. The doors unlock and she runs outside to freedom.)

(MUSIC: A taste of freedom that settles into a melancholy version of the jazzy "Newspaper" theme.)

Scene Twenty: Pulitzer's Office

(SOUND: A muffled newspaper office. A knock on door.)

PULITZER: State your business.

(SOUND: Door opening. Outer office louder, underneath.)

COCKERILL: She's here. Lookin' much better.

PULITZER: Still goin' on about the seven day, ten day thing?

COCKERILL: I told her it was just a little mix up ... she seems to have calmed down on that one.

PULITZER: Good, send her in.

(SOUND: Steps into the office, a rustling skirt, a chair pulled up.)

Nellie! Sit down. How are ya?

NELLIE: Don't look at me like that. I'm not crazy.

(SOUND: The door closes, muffling the outer office.)

PULITZER: I'm not looking at you any special way. You just gave us a scare, that's all—

NELLIE: I got you a great story, didn't I?

(SOUND: He lights a cigar.)

PULITZER: *(Puffing.)* Sold more papers in two days than we usually do in a week. Hey! Did ya hear about the inquiry? The officials are lookin' into Blackwell's Island, there's going to be changes. You did that.

NELLIE: What kind of changes?

PULITZER: They're talking three million dollars worth.

NELLIE: *(Perking up.)* It's about time. Intrepid girl reporter does a little good in a sea of bad.

PULITZER: What? How much time do you want off? … Nellie?

NELLIE: I don't need any time off. I've got lots more stories to tell. *(Picking up speed.)* There's that guy down south with the Wild West Show, Buffalo Bill. Or those shysters up in the garment district—

PULITZER: Now you're talking.

(MUSIC: A jazzy version of the "Insanity" theme, underneath.)

NELLIE: I've got ideas springing from my brain … I always thought I could beat Phileous Fogg, you know "Around the World in Eighty Days?" I could …

(MUSIC: The "Insanity" theme builds with the "Shuffling Feet" theme, swells to a climax and abruptly ends.)

The Duchess

Pieces of Wallis Simpson

by

Linda Griffiths

The Duchess: Pieces of Wallis Simpson was commissioned by the Canadian Broadcasting Corporation for Studio '93, and first broadcast on the CBC Stereo network on March 19, 1993, with the following cast:

Linda Griffiths (Wallis)
Charlie Tomlinson (Edward / Male Four)
Pat Hamilton (Aunt Bessie / Reporter Three)
Paul Bettis (Lord Brownlow / Frederique)
Eric Peterson (Noel / Society Chorus)
Cynthia Eastman (Countess / Society Chorus)
Robert Persichini (Count / Male One)
Karen Kenedy (Operator One / Operator Two / Female / Society Chorus)
Andrew Scorer (Male Two / Reporter Two)
Michael Healy (Male Three / Reporter One)

Produced and directed in Toronto by Baņuta Rubess. Original music by Nic Gotham. Casting Consultant: Linda Grearson. Recording Engineer: John Marynowicz. Sound effects by Joe Hill. Production Assistant: Nancy McIlveen. Script Editor: Ann Jansen. Executive Producer of Studio '93: Bill Lane.

Introduction

For six years I have been fascinated with Wallis Simpson. The story of her life as the North American commoner who toppled the throne of England seems even more outrageous today than in 1937. Her journey to London to become the Prince of Wales's mistress, her transformation to the Duchess of Windsor after the abdication of Edward VIII, and their terrifying life in exile as ex-King and consort contains the elements of all great stories. Wallis Simpson lived a decadent life, beset by nightmares of revenge, jewels as big as golf balls, tied to a dependant ex-King who had never picked up his socks or made a living. A man who "gave up a kingdom" for her.

Why Wallis? I like climbers, I like outrageous women, I like stories where a lot happens. Of course, there's the North American fascination with royalty. Wallis Simpson thought that a king could do anything. Her belief in the powers of monarchies came from the naivete of someone from a democracy. She thought that if Edward VIII really wanted to marry a commoner, all he had to do was "stand up to them" and say so. Then the shit hit the fan in a really big way, and she found herself face to face with the Archbishop of Canterbury, British tradition and the truly obsessive love of one man.

I wanted to create the world the Duchess lived in, to find the style, the decadence, and to expose the ludicrousness of a continuing aristocracy. It's an ugly world, but I wanted to expose it with fun—admitting that we love decadence and have a vicarious relationship to the British monarchy that feeds our colonial perversity. In a time of austerity, I found myself disappearing into photographs of Wallis's huge emeralds, catlike pins, curving jumbles of diamonds and sapphires. A world where "courage" could mean daring to wear severe black to a society ball. I believe Wallis had courage of a kind. She was the one who said, "I can face anything with a manicure and a good cut." A warped world, no doubt.

In this piece, there is a central question. Did Wallis Simpson "love" the ex-King? Even though these stories are about the adventures of big girls, this woman's story is defined by her relationship to this man. If Wallis hadn't got herself mixed up with the Prince of Wales, there would have been a very different story, probably one in which the CBC would not be interested—but who knows? In the "love story of the century," the question of love is all important.

Many people, including Wallis at times, considered the Duke (the ex-Edward VIII) a fool for abdicating. Once Wallis realized the huge repercussions of his marrying her, she would have been quite happy to be royal mistress and watch while Edward married a suitable virgin. Seen in the context of current events concerning his nephew, Prince Charles, Edward VIII seems prophetic and even heroic. He refused to marry someone he didn't love and have Wallis "on the side"—it cost him his job. The fact that he was unquestionably a dependant personality and "needed" a dominatrix in his life, doesn't erase the integrity of his stand.

Rumours and nasty stories about Wallis abound. There is an entire book which tries to prove she was a Nazi spy, and certainly she was in thin water a lot of the time. She was on a dozen surveillance lists. If there is scandal at the present time to do with the Royal Family, imagine 1935, when Queen Victoria still seemed to rule. In Wallis Simpson we find a woman with huge energy, passion, anger, humour, bitchery, ingenuity and intelligence. The power that could have run a mega-business in another age was harnessed to one unfocussed activity: climbing. How far could she get? And the top is the King … isn't it? After the abdication, she created her kingdom in exile with the ferocity of a downed animal. She invented a world where her ex-King would not look like a fool. She would say, of course, "You can never to be too rich, or too thin." But with Wallis, it always seemed to come down to one thing: did she really love him?

LINDA GRIFFITHS

Characters

WALLIS: Wallis Simpson

SOCIETY CHORUS

EDWARD: King Edward VIII

OPERATOR ONE

AUNT BESSIE: Wallis's aunt

MALE ONE, MALE TWO, MALE THREE, MALE FOUR and FEMALE: Crowd members

LORD BROWNLOW: A representative of Buckingham Palace

REPORTER ONE, REPORTER TWO and REPORTER THREE

OPERATOR TWO

NOEL: Noel Coward, the playwright

COUNTESS and COUNT

FREDERIQUE: A servant

The Duchess

Pieces of Wallis Simpson

Scene One: The Salon 1936

(SOUND: Radio static wows in and out underneath the intro music.)

(MUSIC: Stately Victorian parlour music wars with American ragtime; ragtime wins. Music continues.)

SOCIETY CHORUS: *(Sung or chanted.)*
She was from Baltimore,
But she had style.
She went through the London scene,
Like a knife through butter,
Like a knife through butter.

No looks to speak of,
No money to spend,
Divorced, strung out and common,
She caught the King
A commoner caught the King
(And she wasn't even young).

A bit of vulgarity is like
A dash of paprika
In a good dish.

WALLIS: *(Narrating.)* When I got to London, they didn't even know what cocktails were. It's no wonder.

(MUSIC: Very traditional Victorian.)

Scene Two: Bedroom in the Prince's Hideaway 1936

(SOUND: The bedsprings of a squeaking bed, with heavy breath-

ing, followed by silence.)

EDWARD: Wallis, the truth is …

WALLIS: Yes?

EDWARD: The truth is, I've never been very good at …

WALLIS: Yes?

EDWARD: Well, there's the tension of being Prince of Wales and …

WALLIS: Your Highness, I'm an American. We're not so stuffy about these things.

EDWARD: Please call me David, all those close to me do.

WALLIS: Sir … David, I'm truly honoured. Please don't think I'm too forward, but, do you like to play games?

EDWARD: What an extraordinary woman you are … Games?

WALLIS: Lots of people do, it's no crime. When do you feel aroused?

EDWARD: Well, when I think about my … Well, my nanny, to tell you the—

WALLIS: That's where we begin.

(MUSIC: Victorian.)

(SOUND: Bedsprings squeaking with vigour, continuing underneath.)

Bad baby! Bad baby! Don't do that again.

EDWARD: *(Excited.)* Oh, please, oh please let me.

WALLIS: Dirty stinking baby with his little dirty weenie in front! You've soiled your nappy! And you know what we do when baby's soiled his nappy?

EDWARD: What do we do? What do we do?

WALLIS: Don't you know?

EDWARD: We get spanked. I think we get spanked.

WALLIS: Right!

(SOUND: A hand spanking bare flesh. Moans and screams of delight and pain.)

EDWARD: Oh please, yes please yes please yes, spank me again!

(SOUND: More whacking and screams.)

WALLIS: You'll never be any good! Never never!

EDWARD: *(Breathing heavily.)* It's true, it's true, I know …

WALLIS: Now say, "I'm the King of England and I can do what I like!"

EDWARD: I'm not King yet you know …

WALLIS: Say it!

EDWARD: I'm the King of England and I can do as I like!

WALLIS: Say it louder!

EDWARD: I'm the King of England and I can do as I like!

WALLIS: Again!

EDWARD: *(Coming to a climax.)* I'm the King of England … I'm the King of England … I'm the King of England and I … can … do … as … I … like!

WALLIS: *(After a silence.)* Would you like a cigarette, sir?

(SOUND: Cigarette case opened; a match is struck.)

EDWARD: *(Smoking.)* Bloody decent of you, Wallis. Very game I must say.

WALLIS: *(Smoking.)* Just a few things I picked up in China.

EDWARD: I feel a little … well … you know …

WALLIS: It's been a privilege, your Royal Highness.

EDWARD: You're a big girl. Aren't you Wallis? Not afraid of anything.

WALLIS: A big strong girl for her little prince.

(SOUND: Radio static.)

(MUSIC: "America the Beautiful" plays as if through a broken radio, builds to next scene.)

Scene Three: Wallis's London Apartment 1936

WALLIS: Hello? Aunt Bessie, are you there?

OPERATOR: *(Static, on phone.)* Ma'am, this is the United States calling.

WALLIS: I know that, we had a connection …

OPERATOR: London, England on the line, ma'am.

AUNT BESSIE: *(On phone throughout.)* Yes, yes, Wallis, can you hear me?

WALLIS: The phone service here is so bad, the English can't make anything work but their mouths.

AUNT BESSIE: Yes, that's better. So Wallis, is it true?

WALLIS: Is what true?

AUNT BESSIE: Don't do that to your Aunt Bessie, I've known you too long.

WALLIS: Yes, I'm seeing him, but everything is very hush-hush here.

AUNT BESSIE: The papers here are full of speculation, are you sure you know what you're doing?

WALLIS: I'm spending time with a lonely sad man.

AUNT BESSIE: Your husband must be pretty lonely and sad right now.

WALLIS: We're getting a divorce.

AUNT BESSIE: The papers are saying the King wants to marry you.

WALLIS: He's not King yet.

AUNT BESSIE: They say he may abdicate.

WALLIS: I don't even know what that means.

AUNT BESSIE: Stop playing games with me Wallis, you're a big girl now.

WALLIS: Oh, aunt Bessie, I don't know, I'm so alone here and I don't have enough money for the right clothes and everyone is so nice to me but they tell me I don't understand the English and I'm being treated like a queen and I like it … It's the most ridiculous adventure that a girl ever …

AUNT BESSIE: But do you love him?

(SOUND: Telephone static.)

(MUSIC: American ragtime, distant and underneath.)

WALLIS: I can't hear you.

AUNT BESSIE: *(Shouting over the static.)* But do you love him?

WALLIS: *(Over static.)* Can you send me a couple of summer dresses, something simple, navy or black with white piping and maybe a little collar? Everything is so expensive here …

AUNT BESSIE: But do you love him?

WALLIS: It's like being in an enchanted world. He's a prince, a real prince.

(SOUND: Static increases.)

AUNT BESSIE: I know dear, but do you …

OPERATOR: I'm sorry we are unable to complete your connection at this time.

(MUSIC: American ragtime up and out.)

Scene Four: Outside Buckingham Palace 1937

(SOUND: Crowd noises, stamping, cheering, milling, ragged singing of "There'll Always Be an England," bells toll; all underneath.)

SOCIETY CHORUS: *(Sung or chanted.)*
They say the King is going to abdicate.
Abdicate. Abdicate.
Because he can't marry the woman he loves.
Loves? Loves?
He's not allowed to love.
But they say he's going to abdicate
Because he can't marry the woman he loves.
She has two husbands living,
A nasty divorce pending,
That woman can't marry the King.
It's a constitutional crisis!
The archbishop's enraged!
The government's engaged,
The crown's in danger,
World War II's a wager!
The King is dying
Long live the King.

Our golden prince.
Damn her to hell.

(SOUND: Crowd noises rise. Bells toll loudly. Flashbulbs.)

MALE ONE: *(With a Cockney accent.)* Don't give in, sir! You marry Mrs. Simpson if you like.

MALE TWO: *(With a Yorkshire accent.)* Who bloody cares if she's divorced. I'd love to be divorced from my wife.

FEMALE: Three cheers for his Royal Highness!

(SOUND: "Hip hip hooray! Hip hip hooray! Hip hip hooray!" Some booing.)

MALE THREE: *(With an upper-crust accent.)* He can't marry her! She is a slut! An adventuress! We won't stand for it! What about his duty to the crown? Down with the King!

FEMALE: It's the love story of the century.

MALE FOUR: She doesn't love him, she just wants to be Queen.

FEMALE: They are in love.

MALE THREE: They are not.

MALE TWO: They are in bloody love.

MALE THREE: They are not.

MALE TWO: They bloody are. Come here and say that.

(SOUND: Scuffling. Some punching. "Owww," "Take that you bugger," "Bloody traitor," etc.)

MALE ONE: Look here! She's running away! Gone to France. Abandoned him. Three cheers for the King!

(SOUND: Crowd chants again, "Hip hip hooray! Hip hip hooray! Hip hip hooray!" The cheering fades into radio static.)

(MUSIC: A madcap "French" theme.)

Scene Five: A Country Road in France 1937

(SOUND: A car travelling quickly through wet lanes, underneath.)

WALLIS: We have to stop. I have to call him. He said to call at four.

LORD BROWNLOW: I don't know if we dare. The reporters are in hot pursuit, Mrs. Simpson.

WALLIS: Lord Brownlow ...

LORD BROWNLOW: Mrs. Simpson, the palace has put me in charge of your care and I—

WALLIS: With all respect to the palace, you could protect me into disaster. The King is desperate, he could panic and make a very bad mistake. Just up ahead. I'll call from this restaurant.

LORD BROWNLOW: Oh, Lord. They're already here.

Scene Six: Outside Restaurant

(SOUND: Mad cacophony of reporters. Cries of "There she is!" "It's her!" Flashbulbs continue throughout.)

REPORTER ONE: Mrs. Simpson! Will the King abdicate?

WALLIS: Of course not. That would be ridiculous.

REPORTER TWO: Mrs. Simpson? Do you expect to become Queen of England?

WALLIS: I have no desire to be Queen.

REPORTER THREE: *(American accent.)* Aw, come on Wallis! Is the whole thing political? How do tensions with Hitler figure in the whole thing?

WALLIS: My friendship for the King includes a desire for peace in our time.

REPORTER TWO: Is this the love story of the century?

WALLIS: I wouldn't know.

REPORTER ONE: Mrs. Simpson! Is that man your gynaecologist?

LORD BROWNLOW: *(Moving off.)* Let us through. The Great War was won on the playing fields of Eton. Let us through, let us through!

(SOUND: Pushing and shoving through the reporters. Opening and shutting of a door. Silence.)

Gynaecologist?

(MUSIC: Short sting completes scene.)

Scene Seven: Inside Restaurant

(SOUND: Phone being dialled. Static on the line.)

WALLIS: Hello? Hello? David? Can you hear me?

(SOUND: Phone static.)

EDWARD: *(On phone throughout, above the static.)* Wallis? Wallis is that you?

WALLIS: I can't hear you. *(Bad French.)* Excusee. Mon connection est n'est pas bon. Operator? Operator?

OPERATOR TWO: *(French accent, above the static.)* Madame? C'est l'Angleterre.

WALLIS: I know it's l'Angleterre but I can't hear …

EDWARD: Wallis?

WALLIS: David?

EDWARD: Wallis?

WALLIS: David?

OPERATOR TWO: Madame? C'est l'Angleterre …

WALLIS: David, it's awful, the things they're saying about me … death threats … Make them stop, tell them they can't …

EDWARD: I know, my darling, I hate them for it.

WALLIS: You have to listen to me. Whatever you do, don't abdica—

EDWARD: They're all against me. I won't dishonour the crown. I am going to abdica—

(SOUND: Extreme wave of static.)

(MUSIC: Bits of music, some Victorian, a little New Orleans jazz, with a slightly weird effect.)

WALLIS: David! Don't abdicate! Do what they're telling you to do. Marry someone suitable and I'll still be there. It's done all the time. I can't be responsible for …

EDWARD: I won't make a sham marriage and "have you on the side." You will be my wife not my mis—

OPERATOR TWO: Excusez! Votre temps est fini. Si vous desirez continuer il faut …

WALLIS: They'll hate me! The whole world will hate me! David, think of it. If you're not King then …

(MUSIC: Montage above the static. Bits of music, some ragtime, "There'll Always Be an England.")

(SOUND: Bits of sound from the crowd outside the palace, "Hip hip hooray for King Edward!")

EDWARD: I can't hear you darling. Wallis?

WALLIS: *(Almost to herself.)* If you're not King then who will you be?

LORD BROWNLOW: Mrs. Simpson! We have to go.

OPERATOR TWO: Si vous desirez continuer, il faut …

(SOUND: Reporters banging down the door. Distant cries from the reporters. Then more static from the phone.)

EDWARD: I love you darling. I can't live without you. If you flee, I'll pursue you to the ends of the earth. It's too late to go back.

(SOUND: Dial tone.)

WALLIS: *(Sobbing.)* No! Don't do it. Don't do it.

(SOUND: The phone receiver falls back on the hook.)

LORD BROWNLOW: *(Slightly off.)* Mrs. Simpson? If I give you a hoist up, can you fit through the bathroom window? I'm sorry but it seems the only reasonable escape route.

WALLIS: Hoist me up. Here's one for the memoirs.

(SOUND: Window opening. Hoisting sounds from LORD BROWNLOW.)

LORD BROWNLOW: There you go … Yes … Just let me get my hand under … Sorry … Yes.

(SOUND: WALLIS grunting.)

Scene Eight: Outside Restaurant

(SOUND: Shouts from LORD BROWNLOW and WALLIS. They fall into some shrubbery.)

LORD BROWNLOW: *(Panting.)* We're free. A narrow escape.

WALLIS: *(Panting.)* I don't think there'll ever be escape for me again.

LORD BROWNLOW: It is rather romantic though, isn't it?

WALLIS: It reminds me of being broke in Seattle.

(SOUND: Static. Excerpts from Edward VIII's abdication speech: "… and I lay down my burden …" leads into:)

(MUSIC: Time passes with a sombre, stately melody, up and underneath.)

Scene Nine: Dinner Party at the Windsors' French Estate 1946

(SOUND: Clinking glasses, plates, pouring wine, dinner party murmurings.)

EDWARD: Now everyone, it's our eighth anniversary and I'd like to propose a toast. To my darling wife, who has stuck with me through thick and thin, to Wallis, the Duchess of Windsor!

ALL: Wallis, the Duchess of Windsor!

WALLIS: He isn't kidding when he says thick and thin. You can never be too rich or too thin.

NOEL: Tell me more about Maxwell's party, Wallis, all the dirty bits, and I'll put them in my next play.

WALLIS: Why Mr. Coward, how can you suggest such a thing. Later, when we're alone.

COUNTESS: Duchess, your pansies are quite exceptional.

WALLIS: In my garden or at my table?

(SOUND: Everyone laughs.)

NOEL: I must be the most famous pansy here. Or is that true? Anyone who likes needlepoint as much as the Duke here …

EDWARD: Nonsense. Needlepoint's a sign of masculinity in royal circles.

NOEL: Exactly my point.

COUNT: Sir, the Countess and I would like to formally thank you for inviting us here on this auspicious occasion.

COUNTESS: We're very honoured.

EDWARD: Our pleasure, Count.

NOEL: Nobody else would come.

EDWARD: That's not true, everyone wants to dine at the Duchess's table ...

NOEL: That's true, what else does she have to do but eat and drink?

WALLIS: And shop, don't forget shop.

COUNTESS: Duchess, what is this? I have never eaten anything so ... so ... sinfully good.

WALLIS: Large white grapes, skinned and peeled, stuffed with Camembert cheese and held together with toothpicks.

NOEL: Something like his Royal Highness here.

WALLIS: That's enough, only I can say things like that.

EDWARD: Wallis, seeing that this is a special occasion, do you think we could, just this once ...

WALLIS: No.

NOEL: Wallis, you do have the most beautiful eyes and the most horrible laugh I've ever ... let's run away together and do terrible things ...

EDWARD: But Wallis ...

WALLIS: No.

EDWARD: Ooh please. Pretty please sweetums?

NOEL: What does he mean?

WALLIS: He wants to talk about the past.

EDWARD: Yes, he does, he wants to talk about the past. Do you remember when I was Prince of Wales and we used to dance till three at Shilly's and they wouldn't dare close till we had gone? That's being royal, eh?

WALLIS: The past is dead, long live the future!

COUNTESS: Duchess, is it true that the royal family won't receive you?

COUNT: Shhhh!

WALLIS: I hate them, I hate every last stuffy, plumped-up, super-crinolined, look-down-their-noses, rotten, filthy, stinking, snotty, righteous British British British one of them.

NOEL: I take it you're using "British" as an insult then.

EDWARD: The Duchess is American to the core.

WALLIS: Don't tell me what the Duchess is! The Duchess is just fine.

COUNT: Of course she is. And it's the anniversary of so many happy …

WALLIS: The whole world wants to know if we're happy. The whole world wants to know if I was worth it.

EDWARD: You are worth a kingdom, my dear, and always will be.

NOEL: Actually, the whole world wants to know if you love him. Then the romantics will believe it was worth it.

EDWARD: Sweetums and I love each other very deeply. We always have, and we always will.

WALLIS: Shut up, you ninny.

EDWARD: Now Wallis, you know you don't mean …

WALLIS: I hate it when you love me like that.

(SOUND: A chair pushed away from the table.)

EDWARD: We're getting a little testy. I think it's time for the dinner entertainment. The Duke of Windsor playing his pipes.

(SOUND: Polite applause.)

(MUSIC: Mournful Scottish bagpipes play underneath the next exchanges.)

WALLIS: I hate the pipes. I hate the goddamn pipes.

COUNTESS: Is it true that you spend millions on clothes?

COUNT: Is it true the Duke stole the crown jewels for you?

COUNTESS: Is it true that you've had three face-lifts?

NOEL: Is it true the Duke's never had an orgasm?

COUNTESS: Is it true the dogs eat off silver plates?

COUNT: Is it true you and the Duke were Nazis?

COUNTESS: Is it true you have a power over him that …

COUNT: A mysterious hold that …

NOEL: A not so mysterious psycho-sexual dominance that …

(MUSIC: The bagpipes slow and collapse windily.)

(SOUND: A chair pulled back to the table.)

EDWARD: *(Moving on.)* We were just in love, that's all. And it got us in a speck of trouble. Isn't that right, my big girl?

WALLIS: Yes, that's right darling. A speck of trouble.

EDWARD: Oh my sweet. I took you into the void, didn't I?

WALLIS: Yes.

COUNTESS: What void?

WALLIS: Where there's no home, no country, no friends, no family, where the cruel whispers around you are even louder than the whispers in your heart. Where the ulcers twist and crumple and eat themselves at night. Where there is no peace, not for an instant, you have to keep it up, keep it up, keep the bloody thing up. The void is where big girls go when they lie. When they're not big girls at all.

NOEL: I'm not being entertained.

COUNTESS: What void?

WALLIS: All right everybody. We're going to be amusing now, we're going to have fun.

COUNTESS: But what void?

COUNT: Be quiet!

(SOUND: Six dogs enter, pugs. Mad barking, snuffling, drooling and asthmatic wheezing, continuing underneath.)

EDWARD: Here they are ... They've come to say goodnight. Now that one's called Disraeli, do you see how he's always frowning?

NOEL: With a face like that, it's so hard to tell. There seem to be hundreds of them.

EDWARD: Just six little mischiefs.

WALLIS: Naughty girl ... That's Davey Crockett, and she's not happy with her supper is she? Look David, look at the way she wants to woo on Noel's shoes. Naughty.

COUNTESS: Oh! It's climbing up my leg!

COUNT: *(Whispering.)* Just put up with it, they did ask us for dinner. Nice dog, nice ... ohh.

EDWARD: He's done it now. Oh yes, he's done it now.

COUNT: No, it's nothing, really ...

WALLIS: Disraeli's done his business all over the Count's ...

COUNT: Really, it's nothing ...

EDWARD: Wipe him down and send him to my tailor's in Paris. See? He knows he's done wrong and Daddy's going to be vewy angwy. Yes, my puggy wug.

(SOUND: Wild barking, more snuffling.)

COUNTESS: I suppose you never had children.

NOEL: Countess, you are a treasure.

COUNTESS: I was just asking …

WALLIS: Frederique?

FREDERIQUE: Yes ma'am?

WALLIS: Give them their treats anyway. And the entree is cold. I've told you about serving too early.

FREDERIQUE: Sorry, ma'am. Yes ma'am. Right away ma'am.

(SOUND: Plates being cleared away angrily, stomping footsteps, a closing door.)

WALLIS: No. I'm unable to have children.

NOEL: Too many abortions?

WALLIS: Noel, you're a dear friend but I'm warning you …

NOEL: Wallis, do you remember the time that fruity Metcalfe …

WALLIS: Oh, don't …

EDWARD: Dear old fruity …

NOEL: At that ridiculous castle …

WALLIS: *(Starting to laugh.)* Oh no …

NOEL: *(Laughing.)* And he turned around and said …

WALLIS: *(Laughing helplessly.)* With that look on his face …

NOEL: *(Convulsed with laughter.)* And then he …

WALLIS: Bent over almost double …

NOEL: Ohhhh stop …

WALLIS: Look everyone, I've got a broom up my bum!

(SOUND: NOEL and WALLIS laugh hysterically, repeating "a broom up his bum" at various points.)

COUNTESS: I don't see what's so …

COUNT: Shhh … they invited us to dinner so be …

COUNTESS: But I don't understand …

WALLIS: Of course not, Countess. Welcome to the Kingdom in Exile. It's mine. I created it. I fought for the breeches on every tight-bummed servant. We rule here, you see, because we can't rule anywhere else. We keep in the news, we answer our letters, we write our memoirs and we dream of paying them back.

EDWARD: Wallis, don't talk about the past.

NOEL: Does this theory make me court jester?

WALLIS: God, how I love homosexual men. That's right. Don't talk about the past. Did I slip? Maybe. Don't talk about the past. It's a modern world, kings are silly.

EDWARD: I just need some work to do. Perhaps you could help, Count. Something useful. I'm trained to diplomacy. I could have stopped the Second World War ... Ally with Mussolini, break the alliance between Italy and Germany, then hit the Bolsheviks ...

NOEL: Perhaps another time, your Highness.

EDWARD: People will always want kings and queens.

COUNTESS: Why?

EDWARD: Because they're in our playing cards, our chess boards and our faerie tales.

COUNTESS: Your story is like a faerie tale.

WALLIS: In a faerie tale you end up with the goods.

EDWARD: Darling, let's forget the meal and dance. That's the ticket, sticky wicket.

NOEL: The love story that shocked the world.

Scene Ten: Salon

(MUSIC: "Ballroom" theme: "Put on a Happy Face," played by one instrument.)

SOCIETY CHORUS: *(Floating over the music.)*
It is true is it true
That the Duke of Windsor is gay as a
Pansy,
Light as a feather,
As he works in his garden,
As he waters azaleas,
His dahlias,
Is it true, is it true, is it true?

Is it true, is it true
That the Duchess of Windsor
Is a Nazi, is a Nazi,
That she slept with Hitler
Under her bed,
That she drank his blood,
That she embroiders swastikas,

That she smuggles secrets,
Is it true, is it true
That the Duchess of Windsor
Is a spy,
Was a Nazi,
Is a spy spy spy?
Is it true?

Scene Eleven: Ballroom Later that Night

(MUSIC: "Ballroom" theme, played by a trio.)

(SOUND: Trotting feet and clinking glasses.)

COUNT: *(Dancing with WALLIS.)* I would like to know something …

WALLIS: They all do.

COUNT: Well, here I am dancing with one of the most …

WALLIS: … fascinating women in the world, yes?

COUNT: Well …

WALLIS: That's the trouble with Europe's fading gentry … no balls. Sorry Count, nothing personal.

COUNT: No offence taken, it's just that …

NOEL: *(Moving on.)* I must cut in. I can't keep my hands off Wallis … I'm convinced she has some secret power and if I'm close enough it will rub off.

WALLIS: Be nicer to the Duke, Noel … If you want to continue to play with me …

NOEL: How *did* you get him?

WALLIS: Oh, for God's sake, not you too.

NOEL: What I really want to know is …

EDWARD: *(Moving on.)* Excuse me Noel, but I must cut in on my wife, as you know, it's our …

NOEL: *(Moving off.)* Anniversary, yes I do remember it being mentioned once or twice …

EDWARD: I love you more tonight than when we first met.

WALLIS: Thank you, darling.

EDWARD: Just "Thank you, darling"?

WALLIS: I love you too. Thank you for the bracelet. Did Cartier's come up with those yellow diamonds finally?

EDWARD: I have to ask you something.

WALLIS: Walk carefully darling … Watch out for the void …

COUNTESS: What void?

EDWARD: Darling, it concerns …

WALLIS: Leave it alone! Just leave it alone, whatever it is!

EDWARD: Did I ruin your life?

WALLIS: Yes!

EDWARD: Wallis …

WALLIS: *(Vehemently.)* You ruined my life! Are you happy now?

(MUSIC: Stops raggedly.)

(SOUND: Embarrassed coughs.)

NOEL: *(Slightly off.)* Don't be silly, Wallis, your life isn't ruined.

EDWARD: But should I have abdicated, Noel? It was the only thing I could do, but still …

NOEL: The thing is old chap, who cares about the abdication, really.

WALLIS: *(Enraged.)* Who said it? I heard it but I don't believe it.

NOEL: Oh, don't be silly, Wallis. He just wanted to know whether or not he should have abdi—

EDWARD: *(In unison with NOEL.)* … should have abdi—

WALLIS: I'll go insane right here if you say it!

EDWARD: I'm the King, I'll say what I want!

COUNTESS: Actually, you're not the King …

NOEL: I'd shut up if I were you, Countess.

WALLIS: You're nothing! A king with no throne is nothing!

EDWARD: Abdicate! Abdicate! Abdicate!

WALLIS: A weak snivelling momma's boy.

EDWARD: Abdicate! Abdicate! Abdicate!

WALLIS: You should have stood up to them! I'd be Queen now, we'd have a bloody life if you'd—!

EDWARD: It was a noble act, but you wouldn't understand that, would you? *(Quoting.)* "He nothing common did or mean, upon that memorable scene."

WALLIS: You ruined my life, you pansy!

(MUSIC: Starts up again and stops almost immediately.)

EDWARD: I abdicated and I was … *(He gags.)*

(SOUND: EDWARD chokes awfully, continuing underneath.)

WALLIS: What is it? You're just doing this to win …

EDWARD: *(Still coughing, choking and gagging.)* No … actually … I think …

COUNTESS: Was it the fish, it could be a fish bone …

COUNT: An uncle of mine died that way.

NOEL: Well, thump him on the back or something …

WALLIS: Oh, no you're not, you're not going to do this …

EDWARD: *(Gagging and choking.)* Sorry, darling … I …

WALLIS: I'll wack that bone out of you.

(SOUND: WALLIS pushes EDWARD down and gets on top of him, thwacking and some throttling.)

EDWARD: *(Ghastly choking.)* Wallis, I … think … I

COUNTESS: He's turning blue. Someone call a doctor.

NOEL: Stick your finger down his throat, for goodness sake.

(SOUND: Static reminiscent of the telephone call from France.)

(MUSIC: Montage of bits and pieces of songs mixed in with the static. Some Victorian, some ragtime. Fred Astaire "Gotta Dance.")

COUNT: Oh my God, he's dying.

WALLIS: No he's not. David? Can you hear me? Don't you dare die before me.

EDWARD: *(Choking.)* Wallis … there's something … I always … wanted to …

WALLIS: What is it? Speak up, David!

(SOUND: Increased static.)

OPERATOR TWO: *(French accent, on phone, very distant.)* I am sorry, your connection is not complete.

EDWARD: Wallis …

WALLIS: David …?

EDWARD: Wallis … do you really … love …

(SOUND: EDWARD emits a gurgle and a truly awful gasp. Silence.)

NOEL: He's faking.

WALLIS: David! I hate you. I'm bored to death by you. How dare you love me so much. Do you hear me? I hate you for loving me, you snivelling thing. You die on me and I'll kill you.

(SOUND: WALLIS growls and reaches into EDWARD's throat. She pulls out the fish bone. Gagging and pulling noises.)

COUNT: She's got it, it's the bone.

NOEL: It's not very big for all this trouble.

EDWARD: Wallis … Wallis!

WALLIS: Give me some wine.

(SOUND: Wine poured. EDWARD gulping, underneath.)

There, are you better now?

EDWARD: Better.

(MUSIC: Ballroom music starts up, softly and tentatively.)

NOEL: It's hard to know when to believe you Wallis.

WALLIS: I thought of all men in the world, you would know.

NOEL: What an extraordinary thing to …

EDWARD: My dear, when I was in extremis, I heard you saying wonderful things to me, like in a dream.

WALLIS: I just said that if you died on me I'd kill you.

EDWARD: What a wit. My big girl. But I'm afraid I've dampened the party spirit.

(MUSIC: Fades away.)

Scene Twelve: The Foyer Even Later that Night

(SOUND: Rustle of coats pulled on.)

COUNT: Well, it's been a splendid evening.

COUNTESS: I just want to know, what void?

(SOUND: The dogs burst in, wild barking, snuffling and drooling.)

FREDERIQUE: Ma'am, is it time for a hot toddy?

NOEL: That butler of yours is a prince, oh, sorry, bad word. Anyway, I'd steal him if I could.

WALLIS: Now, Churchill, calm down, mummy's here.

EDWARD: There was nothing else I could do but give up the throne for you, you know that.

WALLIS: Yes, I know darling, it was very noble of you.

COUNT: Well, thank you again.

COUNTESS: Oh, and happy anniversary.

(SOUND: A heavy door opening, night sounds.)

NOEL: Countess, you're a treasure. Next time, Wallis, let's gamble all night and lose lots of money.

WALLIS: It's a deal … and Noel?

NOEL: Yes?

WALLIS: Nothing. Take care.

NOEL: And you.

(SOUND: Footsteps off. The door shuts. The dogs snuffle.)

WALLIS: Actually, I think that went very well.

EDWARD: Nighty night darling.

WALLIS: Yes, nighty night.

Scene Thirteen: Wallis's Bedroom 1974

(MUSIC: Finale with occasional bagpipes, underscoring WALLIS.)

WALLIS: *(Internal.)* The fifth year I really couldn't bear him. And the seventh, I think the seventh we were actually quite good friends. And then the eleventh year I was in love with someone else and tortured him dreadfully. And the fifteenth year I thought I would smother him to death with his knitting. The eighteenth year, I ignored him completely. The twentieth year was all right, I guess, except we fought for six months solid. The twenty-third year we were companionable, both of us realizing we were old and no one else would have us. Then he got sick and I had to be good. It wasn't until the morning after he'd gone when I woke up, looked at my face in the mirror, and tried to put my make-up on. It wouldn't stick. I applied it again and again but it just streaked and beaded up. And I realized I love him more than anything on earth. When it didn't matter whether anyone believed me or not.

(MUSIC: Finale out.)

(SOUND: Static.)

No.

Here Comes Ulrike Meinhof

by

Baņuta Rubess

No. Here Comes Ulrike Meinhof was commissioned by the Canadian Broadcasting Corporation for Studio '93, and first broadcast on the CBC Stereo network on March 26, 1993, with the following cast:

Tanja Jacobs (Ulrike)
Joanne Anka (herself)
Barbara Gordon (Policewoman Two / Claudia)
Mark Christmann (Inspector / Librarian)
Oliver Dennis (Röhl / Biff / Policeman One)
Nadia Ross (Gudrun / Mother / Policewoman One)
Peter Outerbridge (BBC / Baader / Policeman Two)
Tom Butler (Comrade / AFN / Man)

Produced and directed in Toronto by Baņuta Rubess. Original music by Victor Bateman. Casting Consultant: Linda Grearson. Recording Engineers: Joanna Anka and John McCarthy. Sound effects by John Stewart. Production Assistant: Kate Nickerson. Script Editor: Ann Jansen. Executive Producer of Studio '93: Bill Lane.

Introduction

During the massive student protests of the late sixties, I was a hotheaded fourteen-year-old living near Frankfurt. In 1970, my sister and I helped organize a general strike at our German high school to fight against the re-institution of the War Measures Act as part of the German legal code. Our teachers condoned our precocious activity, themselves radicals. The entire school listened to the parliamentary debates on the act on the radio. They passed the bill. We lost the battle. A shadow of Nazi Germany had returned to the government.

It was easy to sympathize with Ulrike Meinhof (1934–1976). In her heyday, she was one of the best-known political journalists in Germany, a radical Barbara Frum. Her moral and political beliefs—along with the temper of the times—led her into a blinding rage. She had witnessed the lies and repression of the Nazi Reich as a child, and she suspected the politicians of the 1960s of leading Germany right back into that nightmare.

The break-up of her marriage, the assassination attempt on her radical friend Rudi Dutschke, and her encounters with Andreas Baader and Gudrun Ensslin let her boil over to the point where she felt "resistance" had to replaced with "action." The "action" became the Red Army Faction, or, as it was known in the popular press, the Baader-Meinhof "gang." They robbed banks, bombed buildings and shot American soldiers. Meinhof and her cohorts argued that they were at war with their government, fighting in the name of the people. Their opponents vilified them as murderous terrorists plaguing a peaceful and democratic society.

Joanne Anka was my sound engineer for many of the plays in this adventure series. Petite and highly competent, as a woman Anka is herself a rarity in a male-dominated field. During one particularly late session at work, she told me stories about ghosts who supposedly haunted our workplace, Studio G.

When I began to write about Ulrike Meinhof, self-proclaimed defender of "the people," I wondered what she would do if she met "the people" in the flesh. This led to thoughts about Joanne. The haunted studio and Ulrike's story blended into one. The result is *No. Here Comes Ulrike Meinhof.*

BAŅUTA RUBESS

Characters

ULRIKE: Ulrike Meinhof

INSPECTOR

CLAUDIA: A wealthy friend of Ulrike

RÖHL: Klaus Rainer Röhl, Ulrike's husband and publisher of the magazine konkret

MOTHER: Ulrike's mother

BBC and AFN: Radio announcers for the British Broadcasting Corporation and the American Forces Network

GUDRUN: Gudrun Ensslin, a member of the Red Army Faction

BAADER: Andreas Baader, nominal co-leader with Ulrike of the Red Army Faction

JOANNE: A radio sound engineer

COMRADE

MAN

POLICEMAN ONE, POLICEMAN TWO, POLICEWOMAN ONE and POLICEWOMAN TWO

BIFF: A maintenance man

No.

HERE COMES ULRIKE MEINHOFF

Scene One: Demonstration Outdoors in Town 1959

(SOUND: A small crowd, serious and quiet. A microphone squeaks as someone tests it.)

ULRIKE: *(On mike.)* Fellow students, fellow Christians. The experts say Hiroshima was not the end of the world. The murder of five and a half million Jews wasn't the end of the world either. We must end the build-up of nuclear arms. We Germans must not be guilty of yet another crime against humanity before God and mankind.

(SOUND: Polite applause.)

Scene Two: Interview Montage

(MUSIC: Driving 1970s-style rock, the "Ulrike" theme, underneath.)

INSPECTOR: She was the toughest case of my career. Her network reached as far as the Japanese Red Army and the Italian Red Brigades.

CLAUDIA: I never dreamed my sunbathing partner would have a prison built especially for *her*.

RÖHL: *(Musing.)* When I married Ulrike, I felt ... proud? When we separated, I felt ... indifferent? And then, after her suicide, I felt ... sad?

INSPECTOR: Meinhof was brought up by women who felt they should have prevented the Third Reich from happening. Her whole generation! Their German inheritance: guilt! Guilt and an irrational fear of the state.

Scene Three: Living-room, May 1945

(SOUND: Bells ring, women cheer, birds chirp.)

ULRIKE: *(As a child.)* Mami, mami, the war is over!

MOTHER: Hitler has capitulated. This means no more fear! No more lies in Germany! Never forget this day, Ulrike, never.

(MUSIC: "Ulrike" theme swells up.)

Scene Four: Montage

INSPECTOR: You see! Trained against the state from the very beginning!

CLAUDIA: She was always so serious. She was our conscience.

RÖHL: Christ, she was still saying grace when I met her! You remember the fifties. When we were all on that anti-atomic death-trip. It was dislike at first sight. For both of us.

(SOUND: Outdoor crowd, as in Scene One, distant. Squeaky microphone, underneath.)

ULRIKE: *(On mike, distant.)* Ulrike Meinhof.

RÖHL: *(On mike, distant.)* Klaus Rainer Röhl.

(Over his microphone voice.) I couldn't stand her type. That deep and earnest look. But then, *she* called me an emetic. Me, an emetic!

CLAUDIA: I certainly found him exasperating.

RÖHL: *(Exasperated.)* No, not an enema, an e-me-tic! Something that makes you vomit! *(False laugh.)* The little puritan.

INSPECTOR: Her marriage to Klaus Rainer Röhl, publisher of the magazine called *konkret*, made them, well, the Charles and Lady Di of radical chic.

CLAUDIA: Klaus got her out of the dark glasses and into Dion and miniskirts right away.

RÖHL: We were invited to all the parties.

CLAUDIA: She was *so* provocative, and she danced *so* well. And we tolerated Klaus.

RÖHL: Rikibaby was the star journalist of West Germany.

INSPECTOR: Even the wife and I watched her on TV.

CLAUDIA: And all of a sudden she's a desperado! *(A peal of laughter.)*

RÖHL: As a mother to our daughters, Ulrike … no comment.

CLAUDIA: It was a time of communes and hippies—throwing eggs at Hubert Humphrey and pudding at Amerika Haus in Berlin—

INSPECTOR: Of course the KGB pulled the strings.

RÖHL: Everything changed when Benno Ohnesorg was shot. When the Shah of Iran came to Berlin. Remember the Shah of Iran?

Scene Five: Magazine Offices, Hamburg 1967

(SOUND: Furious typewriter, underneath.)

AFN: ... the Shah of Iran arrives in Berlin today, with the Empress Farah Diba. You have been listening to the American Forces Network.

(MUSIC: "A Whiter Shade of Pale" on the radio, underneath.)

(SOUND: Typewriter stops, a paper is pulled out.)

RÖHL: *(Reading out loud, overlapping after first few words of radio broadcast.)* "Open letter to Farah Dibah ... torture is an everyday event of Persian justice." Vintage Meinhof, Ulrike.

ULRIKE: Our government! Inviting this Shah, this criminal.

RÖHL: Jürgen is bringing tomatoes to the march. And I'll bring the cognac. Or would you rather smoke hash? I'll bring both.

ULRIKE: I told you, Klaus, I'm staying in Hamburg for the weekend.

RÖHL: Why? The pigs won't arrest us. Your articles are too dangerous. *(Chuckle, then sighs.)* All right, all right, stay at home with the twins.

Scene Six: Interview Montage

(MUSIC: "Ulrike" theme.)

INSPECTOR: She'd had an operation for a brain tumour.

RÖHL: She had a fear of crowds.

CLAUDIA: Oh, that was the day we went shopping. She found a darling Tiffany lamp.

Scene Seven: Demonstration

(SOUND: Chants of "Shah, Shah, Charlatan" build and lead to screams, shots, sirens. Murmuring grows in the crowd.)

GUDRUN: *(Calling.)* The pigs killed a student! Shot him in cold blood!

(SOUND: Furious typing, underneath.)

AFN: *(On radio, underneath.)* You've been listening to the American Forces Network.

ULRIKE: A loud bang on June the 2nd, 1967. The murder of twenty-six-year-old Benno Ohnesorg attending his first demonstration, the devout Protestant newlywed expecting his first child, the acquittal of the police sergeant responsible—

(SOUND: Typing fades underneath.)

INSPECTOR: It brought out the latent paranoia in all of them. Gudrun Ensslin, later Meinhof's partner in crime, and of course, Andreas Baader …

(MUSIC: A paranoid guitar segue to next scene.)

Scene Eight: Student Sit-in, Auditorium

(SOUND: Student crowd, hubbub about Ohnesorg.)

GUDRUN: *(Sobbing.)* Andreas, it's the Auschwitz generation … those old Nazis will kill us all if we don't get them first.

BAADER: They're all fascistoid shits in a police shit-state.

(MUSIC: Wild guitar, up and underneath.)

(SOUND: Police siren and explosions.)

BBC: April 2, 1968. Explosions in Frankfurt department stores as a protest against the war in Vietnam. Gudrun Ensslin and Andreas Baader are accused of setting fire bombs in the furniture department of Kaufhaus Schneider—

INSPECTOR: *(Overlapping the last few words of BBC.)* First it's pudding, then it's fire bombs!

Scene Nine: Prison

(SOUND: Footsteps down a concrete hallway, the swing of a prison door, a chair drawn to a table.)

ULRIKE: Ulrike Meinhof, *konkret*. I hope the prison guards are treating you well.

GUDRUN: At least one of them's cute.

ULRIKE: Frau Ensslin, our readers agree with you in theory. But—

GUDRUN: Theory! *(Laughs raucously.)*

(MUSIC: Tingles along, taking us to:)

(SOUND: Footsteps down a concrete hallway, the swing of a prison door, a chair drawn to a table.)

ULRIKE: Herr Baader, in theory I am sympathetic to—

BAADER: Theory! *(Raucous laughter.)*

ULRIKE: Herr Baader, arson in department stores is not really anti-capitalist, arson only increases the profit margin.

BAADER: Frau Meinhof. Are you frigid?

Scene Ten: Montage

(MUSIC: Punctuates the following.)

AFN: May 14, 1970. Berlin. On a prison pass to the library, arsonist Andreas Baader leaps to freedom. In a daring escape engineered by journalist Ulrike Meinhof, the convicted criminal …

BBC: *(Overlapping AFN; begins at "Meinhof".)* … unlocked his handcuffs. Andreas Baader jumped from the window, followed by journalist Ulrike Meinhof. A reward of ten thousand Deutschemark has been offered by the authorities for information leading to their …

RÖHL: *(Overlapping the last few words of BBC.)* Hell, by that time, we hadn't spoken for months.

CLAUDIA: Klaus and his eternal girlfriends. Ulrike ran off to Berlin, and we lost touch.

INSPECTOR: Baader and Ensslin had skipped parole since that fire-bomb thing, wandered around Europe, returned to Berlin, showed up on Meinhof's doorstep. We caught Baader, put him safely behind bars and—she came to the rescue.

RÖHL: It was so terribly romantic, and so very logical. Joan of Arc! … Pathetic!

INSPECTOR: Meinhof, Baader, Ensslin. They went underground for a year. Rumour had it she was dead.

CLAUDIA: We all have that mid-life crisis.

AFN: October 22, 1971. Hamburg. Traffic cop shot during a routine check. A group calling itself the Red Army Faction, otherwise known as the Baader-Meinhof gang has claimed …

BBC: *(Overlapping.)* … the Red Army Faction, otherwise known as the Baader-Meinhof gang. Ulrike Meinhof, former journalist, is thought to be the leader of the group which includes …

INSPECTOR: *(Overlapping the last few words of BBC.)* Meinhof was the *political* mastermind—Baader and Ensslin were the—

AFN: May 11, 1972. Frankfurt. Three bombs in the U.S. Army headquarters caused the death of Lieutenant Colonel Paul Bloomquist, wounding thirteen others.

BBC: May 12, 1972. Augsburg. Two bombs exploded in the police headquarters, wounding five policemen. A car exploded two hours later in the ...

RÖHL: *(Overlapping the last few words of the radio.)* I couldn't believe it. She was afraid of guns, she wept hysterically when—

BBC: *(Overlapping.)* ... ten people were wounded when the cars exploded in the parking lot of the State Criminal Investigation Office. The damages are estimated at ...

AFN: *(Overlapping.)* ... destroying the car completely. The victim is the wife of the federal judge handling the Baader-Meinhof case. Severely crippled, Mrs. Wolfgang Buddenberg automatically triggered the bomb when she ...

BBC: *(Overlapping.)* Bombs exploded in the Springer Press building, injuring seventeen employees. Calling themselves Commando Benno Ohnesorg, Meinhof's gang has accused the publishing house of ignoring their warnings.

RÖHL: Why do they insist it was suicide? All the evidence points to the contrary.

CLAUDIA: Ulrike loved life, she—

INSPECTOR: She was not murdered by the police!

AFN: According to the police, the latest tally is four dead and seventy-four wounded.

INSPECTOR: No!

BBC: The Baader-Meinhof gang have become Germany's Public Enemy Number One in this war of six against sixty million.

CLAUDIA: Eight months in isolation in a bare white cell, fluorescent lights that are never turned off, absolute silence, absolute sensory deprivation. *Mon dieu,* I'd kill myself too.

(MUSIC: Abruptly changes to digital noise, then out.)

Scene Eleven: Studio G

JOANNE: What the ...? Oh Christmas crackers.

(SOUND: Buttons being pushed.)

(Close.) Um ... please stand by for, uh, technical difficulties ... um you're listening to the CBC ... damn!

(SOUND: The creak of a chair, buttons being pushed, a phone ringing.)

(Muttering.) Come onnnn, maintenance, pick it uuup.

ULRIKE: *(Through radio crackling, barely audible.)* ... the progressive element here is in the breaking of the law ...

(SOUND: Other party picks up the phone.)

BIFF: *(On phone.)* Maintenance. Biff here.

JOANNE: Hi, it's Joanne Anka up in Studio G?

BIFF: *(On phone.)* Biff.

JOANNE: Hi, Biff. I'm running a drama down here and it suddenly conked out. And I think I'm on air. I think a hundred thousand listeners are getting the sound engineer right now.

BIFF: *(On phone.)* I think if you checked the listings again—

JOANNE: Okay, ten thousand. I don't care if it's a couple of hundred, this is an emergency.

BIFF: *(On phone.)* I don't know what to do.

JOANNE: Then check the manual.

ULRIKE: *(Wafting in strongly.)* The state is lawless. The people must wage war against the state.

JOANNE: And the air conditioning is on the fritz, it's suddenly freezing. Nothing works here any more. *(Off the phone.)* Hey, who let you in here!

(SOUND: Phone drops, electric sparkle of a thousand wires as Ulrike Meinhof's ghost transubstantiates in Studio G. In the beginning, ULRIKE is very calm and reasonable, even when saying the most unreasonable things. She knows she's dead, but the world hasn't changed since 1976.)

ULRIKE: *(Very close.)* Members of the oppressed—

JOANNE: *(Over.)* I didn't see you come in—

ULRIKE: —people of the Third World—

JOANNE: *(Over.)* Get off that mike!

ULRIKE: *(To JOANNE.)* I'm making a broadcast.

JOANNE: No, you're not! Boy, the security in this building!

ULRIKE: *(Over.)* Working mothers who can't pay their rent, teenage drop-outs who can't find a job: Commando Ulrike Meinhof of the Red Army Faction has occupied—

(SOUND: Wrestling with the mike, underneath.)

JOANNE: I'm going to ... have to ask you to leave the studio.

ULRIKE: *(To JOANNE.)* I have a gun and I will shoot.

JOANNE: Pardon?

ULRIKE: A gun. A Firebird. An excellent pistol. It shoots right through the car door.

JOANNE: *(Stunned.)* That's a gun.

ULRIKE: Good. *(Very close.)* Members of the oppressed. *(To JOANNE.)* Where am I?

JOANNE: Studio G. You know. Studio G, CBC. Toronto, Ontario, Canada, planet Earth, whatever.

ULRIKE: We address you from the colony of American imperialism, Toronto. We object to this broadcast. We have taken the studio and its workers hostage and will not release them until the truth is told.

(SOUND: The telephone rings and is picked up very quickly. JOANNE dives under a table.)

BIFF: *(On phone.)* Maintenance. Biff here.

JOANNE: *(Whispering.)* Biff, hurry, call 911, I'm under a table, there's a lady in here with a gun and—

BIFF: *(On phone.)* Very funny.

JOANNE: I'm not joking! There's a lady—*(Loud.)* Don't shoot!

Don't ...

(SOUND: Rustle of clothes; JOANNE rising.)

Don't ... *(Into the phone.)* Honestly, this really wacko lady was here. Sure, I'll call security right away ...

BIFF: *(On phone.)* I still don't know what to do.

JOANNE: Right. Well, when you find the manual. *(Afterthought.)* And it's still freezing!

(SOUND: The telephone is hung up.)

ULRIKE: *(Hissing.)* No more phone calls, Joanne Anka.

JOANNE: *(Yelps.)* Okay, this is not funny. Just quit with the appearing and disappearing whoever you are.

ULRIKE: I have a statement to make, dammit.

JOANNE: Okay, okay, you don't have to be rude.

ULRIKE: I see. It's not rude to drop napalm on innocent people. But it *is* rude to make a political statement.

JOANNE: You know, somebody out there *is* listening and they'll call the police.

ULRIKE: Good. I want them to listen. I have a Firebird. And in my bag I have one sub-machine-gun, two hand-grenades, and one ten-pound bomb. So, now, play "A Whiter Shade of Pale"!

JOANNE: What?!

ULRIKE: Okay, "Tommy" by The Who.

JOANNE: There's no music in this studio. I'd have to go downstairs.

ULRIKE: *(Sharply.)* You are not leaving this room. What about those tapes on the floor?

(SOUND: Rummaging through tapes, a tape being loaded.)

JOANNE: *(Muttering.)* "Morningside" must have left them. It's such a mess in this place …

(MUSIC: Theme from "Morningside," CBC Radio's national morning program, underneath.)

ULRIKE: *(Very intimate)* My friends. You need a new coat. You need a new dental floss. New toys from Mattel. Your children scream for them until you beat them. No one knows you beat them. I do. You just bought a new hi-fidelity system from RCA. Now it's obsolete. You need a new one. You just bought new nylons. Now they have a run. You need new ones. You don't know about torture and the Shah of Iran, but you know the subtle difference between cars and detergents and baby foods. I looked through all of Hamburg for a particular Tiffany lamp and it Just! Wasn't! There! I need a new one. This is what is called the terror of consumption. You think you are happy and contented but you're not. You are a slave to the commercials on the television. You are a slave to all those things that you must buy. You are the helpless object of corporate interests living in a fascistic state. You don't have a life. You have a wallet. And it blinds you to the fact that people are dying in Vietnam, the Americans are bombing peaceful villages, women and children writhing from the wounds inflicted by—Change this music, bitch! Change this music! You are trying to kill me with this music!

(MUSIC: "Morningside" theme out.)

I asked you to get me "A Whiter Shade of Pale." Play "A Whiter Shade of Pale" and you won't get hurt.

JOANNE: *(Very frightened!)* If you want me to … I'd have to go to the music library.

ULRIKE: I need a cigarette, bitch! Give me a cigarette!

JOANNE: This is a no-smoking zone. There is a fine if you—

ULRIKE: Cigareeeeettttes! Cigareeeetttttes!

JOANNE: If you want … I can go to the cafeteria. There's always somebody … in the cafeteria …

ULRIKE: I have children too, you know. I gave up my children to fight for the people. Now. Play "A Whiter Shade of Pale."

JOANNE: I told you, I—

ULRIKE: What are all these tapes on the shelf, huh?! Huh?!

(SOUND: Rummaging.)

JOANNE: Sound effects. You won't like it.

ULRIKE: No, play it!

JOANNE: *(Muttering, over.)* Okay, you're the boss.

(SOUND: Loading of a cassette. Sound effects explosions, underneath.)

ULRIKE: *(Pacing.)* And it's not a brain tumour, it's a blood clot. There is a wire clamping a vein in my head, but the effect is purely physical. And I refuse to be X-rayed again! Your death is meaningless, but mine …! Do you know who I am?! A hundred thousand readers devour every one of my columns, even when I have nothing to say. But I say it so passionately.

JOANNE: So you're a journalist? Is this a stunt?

(SOUND: The phone rings.)

ULRIKE: If you answer the phone, I'll shoot.

JOANNE: Fine. I'm not answering.

ULRIKE: Good. *(Pause.)*

(SOUND: Phone rings irritatingly.)

JOANNE: You made your statement. What else do you want?

ULRIKE: They must release all the prisoners. They must blow up the stores. They must bring us some music. Or else I will shoot. I will shoot. I will—*answer the goddamn phone, bitch!*

(SOUND: Sound effects out. The phone picked up.)

JOANNE: Hello, Studio G, Joanne Anka, help, hello, Biff.

BIFF: *(On phone.)* Uh, is it fixed?

JOANNE: No, *(Through clenched teeth.)* just listen!!

BIFF: *(On phone.)* It isn't fixed?

JOANNE: No, nothing's been fixed yet—*if you listened!!* You—

BIFF: *(On phone.)* I don't know what to do.

JOANNE: The back of the manual. Look under override.

ULRIKE: *(Hissing.)* Music. And cigarettes.

JOANNE: *(To ULRIKE.)* Biff doesn't smoke. *(To BIFF.)* Yeah, could you ask Bernie for a music tape? "Whiter Shade of Pale," whatever that is. Oh and when you do, could you bring me a coffee? I'm stuck in the studio, and ... double double.

BIFF: *(On phone.)* Double double.

JOANNE: Thanks.

(SOUND: The phone is hung up.)

ULRIKE: And now you lock the door. Bernie is not coming in here to throw hot coffee in my face.

JOANNE: Biff. He won't throw coffee.

ULRIKE: No, *you* will, you think I'm stupid? Lock the door.

(SOUND: Door being locked.)

JOANNE: I wasn't planning anything, I'm just really cold.

ULRIKE: Sure. Then here, take my jacket.

(SOUND: Jacket being pulled off, flung across room and caught.)

JOANNE: *(On the verge of tears.)* Thanks.

(SOUND: Jacket being pulled on.)

ULRIKE: Joanne Anka. Like Paul Anka?

JOANNE: Yeah. It's Syrian, actually.

ULRIKE: I drove through Syria once.

JOANNE: I've never been to Syria.

ULRIKE: We working mothers are all the same. We know what it's like to suffocate from the children and the lies, we know how we feel when we throw plates at our husbands, when we shut the windows before we scream that we just can't stand it any more.

JOANNE: Yeah. Um. Actually, I'm not married.

ULRIKE: *That's a detail!* I am just like you. We are women. You know my ex-husband, you've seen the photos, the chest, the hair, the gold chains, Klaus Rainer Röhl thinks he's Herr Hugh Fucking Hefner. *(Scene Twelve suddenly blaring, ULRIKE continues underneath.)* What's that! What's that—?!

JOANNE: *(Underneath.)* It's the drama! Maintenance fixed it!

ULRIKE: *(Underneath.)* Well, turn it off! Turn it off!

Scene Twelve: An Outdoor Training Camp in Jordan

(MUSIC: Militaristic version of "Ulrike" theme.)

(SOUND: Distant pistol training. A small commando running.)

BAADER: Jordan is a shit-hole. I had better food in prison.

GUDRUN: It's a military camp, not a spa, Andreas baby.

BAADER: The glorious El Fatah! These Palestinian resistance fighters are so uptight.

COMRADE: *(Moving on.)* Comrades! We try again this morning with Comrade Meinhof. But I cannot say the woman has talent.

GUDRUN: Don't give us this patriarchal crap. Ulrike has never seen a hand-grenade before. It's your job to teach her how to use it. And stop staring at my tits.

COMRADE: You have tits, Comrade Ensslin? *(Moving off.)* Comrade Meinhof! This way!

ULRIKE: *(Calling, off.)* Salaaaaam!

GUDRUN: *(Calling.)* Good luck, Ulrike.

BAADER: We should dump her.

GUDRUN: We can't. Her face is plastered on wanted posters all over Germany.

COMRADE: *(Distant.)* You take the hand-grenade. Take it in your hand.

BAADER: She's holding it like it's a dead chicken or something. Like it's a limp, dripping dick.

(SOUND: GUDRUN giggles.)

COMRADE: *(From a distance.)* Now you pull the pin—

BAADER: I thought we agreed she would get me into the library, I would jump out the window and she'd stay behind and play the innocent.

GUDRUN: Well, she didn't. And Peter shot the librarian.

BAADER: He'll live.

GUDRUN: Ulrike will supply the theory and we'll supply the—

COMRADE: Throw the grenade—throw it away—throw it!

GUDRUN: Oh, no, shit!

COMRADE, GUDRUN and BAADER: *(Running away.)* You throw it awaaaay!

(SOUND: Explosion in the sand.)

Scene Thirteen: Studio G

(SOUND: Buttons being pushed.)

JOANNE: I have to find … he's using the override.

Scene Twelve (reprise): Jordan

COMRADE, GUDRUN, BAADER: *(Running away.)* You throw it awaaay!

(SOUND: Explosion in the sand.)

ULRIKE: *(Running up.)* I knew I had to throw it, but I was somehow completely paralysed.

BAADER: You're a useless slut.

(MUSIC: "Ulrike" theme, anguished.)

INSPECTOR: Even if her function was mainly one of propaganda, the weapons in her possession were enough to—

Scene Thirteen (cont.): Studio G

JOANNE: I stopped it. Okay? I'd feel a lot better if you put that gun down.

ULRIKE: *(Tired and depressed.)* I'm not concentrating. I can't concentrate. I pissed my soul away. My brain is stewed fruit. I need an aspirin.

JOANNE: I might have some in my bag.

ULRIKE: *(Listlessly.)* Don't touch that bag or I'll shoot.

(SOUND: The squeak of a chair, rummaging in a bag.)

JOANNE: Sorry, no ... but hey, I've got some cassettes. And a tuna and walnut sandwich.

ULRIKE: It's poisoned. I refuse to eat it.

JOANNE: Suit yourself.

(SOUND: Sandwich is unwrapped.)

(Munching.) I've got these great cover versions of—oh! You'll like this one!

(SOUND: Cassette being loaded.)

(Muttering) ... freezing!

(MUSIC: Bruce Cockburn's "If I Had A Rocket Launcher.")

ULRIKE: I'm just looking for warmth, I'm looking for people, for a group, for a community ...

JOANNE: *(Very sympathetic.)* Sure, of course you are. Was this Ulrike a friend of yours?

ULRIKE: I wrote all the pamphlets, I had all the contacts ...

Scene Fourteen: Ulrike's Kitchen, 1967

(MUSIC: Tragic "Ulrike" theme, in mid-phrase.)

CLAUDIA: ... so many contacts. But the private hell was something else.

(SOUND: Children crying, bacon sizzling on the stove, underneath.)

RÖHL: *(Threatening.)* Rikibaby. Put that pan down or you'll be very sorry.

ULRIKE: Not in front of the children, Klaus.

RÖHL: I think I should teach you a lesson.

Scene Fifteen: Studio G

(MUSIC: "If I Had a Rocket Launcher" abruptly returns.)

JOANNE: It's either Biff or the equipment, I can't figure it out.

ULRIKE: This broadcast must be stopped immediately. I have lectured at the Institute of Media Studies at the Free University of Berlin on the

Possibility of Agitation and Education in Radio Features and this drama is a crime.

JOANNE: I guess the writer got the facts wrong.

ULRIKE: Facts are irrelevant. The people need the truth.

JOANNE: I work on so many of these dramas I don't even listen any more. It's up to the producers to check the facts.

ULRIKE: Not the facts, the truth.

JOANNE: But the facts *are* the truth.

(MUSIC: "If I Had a Rocket Launcher" stops.)

ULRIKE: *This* is the truth. I am a prisoner of war. I am fighting a war on your behalf. I, Ulrike Meinhof. You watched me on television. That was theory, that was babbling, that was crap. *Action* is what matters. *This* is action. I am taking *you* hostage, wake up and say *"No!"*

JOANNE: *(Underneath.)* Okay, no. I'm saying "No." ... Hey—*(Singsong.)* No-oh.

ULRIKE: *(Ranting.)* Is anybody listening? Anybody? Freedom of the press, hah! The announcer's reports on napalm bombs and Elizabeth Taylor's face lifts are in exactly the same voice. He talks of children starving in the slums and reads the weather report with exactly the same look on his face. A pig shoots an innocent student and the pig walks free. But I, Ulrike Meinhof, I'm supposed to be your enemy. Don't you understand? They are trying to put you to sleep. To persuade you that the government controls everything. That politics is fate. Your only defence is to blow it all up.

JOANNE: *(Dawning realization.)* You really think you're Ulrike Meinhof.

ULRIKE: I *am.* And I am telling you, Joanne Anka, *you must change the world! You must make them listen, or else!* ... Or else ... you will lose your children and your parents will die and your husband will sleep around with women from politically volatile countries and the state will kill you and everyone who has a right to be human before God and mankind.

JOANNE: Well, I just said "No" and nothing happened. And I think you're tired and upset and you should lie down. And we should all go home and change the world—tomorrow.

ULRIKE: I see. Okay. You cow. Your Gestapo tactics won't work with me!

Scene Sixteen: Wealthy Dinner Party

(MUSIC: Muzaky, something like "The Girl from Ipanema.")

(SOUND: Clink of glasses and cutlery, appreciative laughter, small talk: "The pheasant is exquisite." "So I said, sell the Jaguar." A phone ring in the distance, the phone is picked up.)

CLAUDIA: We were just talking about you! Mario made pheasant just the way you like it. No, silly, the phone isn't tapped.

(SOUND: Muffled talk in the room.)

Günter Grass says to come over and dance with him. *(Beat.)* Well, you know I support you, Ulrike, but this is illegal!! You know what?! I'll give you my Mercedes, it's just a plain old thing.

(MUSIC: Muzak dips and continues underneath next scene.)

Scene Seventeen: Studio G

ULRIKE: Can't you stop this drivel, damn it?

JOANNE: *(Angrily.)* Just let me go. I never did anything to you!

(SOUND: A tape rewinding at high speed.)

Scene Eighteen: The Library

(MUSIC: "Ulrike" theme, tense.)

(SOUND: A creaky door, arriving steps, murmurs.)

LIBRARIAN: Welcome to the library, sir.

BAADER: I'm afraid I can't shake your hand.

ULRIKE: Officer, remove his handcuffs, we can't work like this.

POLICEMAN: Well … all right, Frau Meinhof.

(SOUND: Handcuffs removed.)

INSPECTOR: It was a betrayal of trust. Meinhof claimed she was writing a book with Baader, about juvenile delinquents.

(MUSIC: "Ulrike" theme up and out.)

Scene Nineteen: Library Table by the Window

(SOUND: Pages turning, birds chirping, a car idling in the distance.)

ULRIKE: *(Whispering.)* Peter will run in with the guns. He won't shoot, of course. We'll distract the pigs, you jump out the window. Astrid is waiting in an Alfa Romeo.

BAADER: *(Whispering.)* I have a hard-on.

ULRIKE: Andreas!

(SOUND: The door bursting open, running steps, moving on.)

(MUSIC: Rush of excitement.)

MAN: Everybody freeze!

LIBRARIAN: Stop!

(SOUND: A gun shot, the librarian is hit. BAADER climbing and jumping out the window, underneath.)

CLAUDIA: They didn't mean to shoot the librarian. And Ulrike was so lonely at the time.

ULRIKE: *(Off.)* I'm coming with you!

(SOUND: ULRIKE climbing and jumping out of the window, a car squeals off.)

RÖHL: Who knows? It was her leap to freedom.

(MUSIC: Cut in mid-crescendo.)

Scene Twenty: Studio G

ULRIKE: Change it.

JOANNE: Change what?!

ULRIKE: I jump out the window. No one is shot. We topple the government. The stores burn to ashes. Get me new actors. I want a new script.

JOANNE: What's the point? It's already been broadcast.

ULRIKE: Change it, bitch! Change it! If you don't change it I'll shoot! I'm dead! I'm dead! Because I jumped to Freeeeeeeedom!

JOANNE: Listen, I just work here.

(SOUND: The door being tried, a knock. With a cry of rage ULRIKE lunges at JOANNE.)

BIFF: *(Muffled.)* Maintenance.

(SOUND: Knocking continues underneath.)

ULRIKE: Don't let them in or I'll show you. I'll take you with me, Commando Ulrike Meinhof. You must honour the dead.

JOANNE: *(Choking.)* Take your hands off ... my ... neck!

(SOUND: With an effort, JOANNE tears herself free, opens the door. Sudden digital noise gets fainter as steps come in.)

(Panting.) Watch out, Biff, she's got a gun. Behind the door!

(SOUND: The door squeaks shut.)

BIFF: Ha ha.

JOANNE: She's gone.

BIFF: Your jacket's on the floor.

JOANNE: That's not my ... jacket.

BIFF: I got that tape. No coffee. Cafeteria's closed.

JOANNE: Oh. Yeah. Thanks.

BIFF: Think we've got it fixed now.

JOANNE: Yeah.

BIFF: Well, bye.

JOANNE: Bye.

(SOUND: The door opening and closing, steps receding.)

Lackey.

(MUSIC: "Ulrike" final theme swells for next scene.)

Scene Twenty-one: Police Station

(SOUND: Struggle as ULRIKE is held down.)

INSPECTOR: This emaciated woman can't possibly be Meinhof. Why, she can't weigh more than ninety pounds.

POLICEWOMAN: Any significant scars, sir?

(SOUND: Clothes being ripped off, ULRIKE swearing at cops.)

INSPECTOR: There's the scar from the Caesarean birth, but that won't identify her conclusively. Hey! The operation! There's that wire in Meinhof's brain.

POLICEWOMAN TWO: We'll X-ray her immediately.

POLICEMAN TWO: Congratulations, Inspector.

INSPECTOR: All of Germany will sleep more easily when they know this wild monster of a woman is safely behind bars.

(SOUND: ULRIKE being carried away.)

ULRIKE: No! No! Nooooo!

(SOUND: Cuts out abruptly.)

Scene Twenty-two: Studio G

(SOUND: Changing of tapes.)

(MUSIC: "A Whiter Shade of Pale" begins and continues underneath closing credits.)